Rude Britannia

'Although everything else in this country may be going down the pan, this book proves that Britain's proud tradition of vulgarity is still in rude health.'
Simon Thorp and Graham Dury, editors of *Viz*

'This is a truly exciting project: it brings the "rude" out into the open, and situates it in oppositionality and cultural conflict. I'm sure this book will provoke readers, in ways that rudeness ordinarily doesn't, as well as educate and entertain.'
Amit Chaudhuri, author of *D. H. Lawrence and 'Difference'*
and Reader at the University of East Anglia

'*Rude Britannia* is one of the most compelling books on British taboos that I have ever read. What made the book essential reading for me was that it doesn't have an ideological axe to grind: while much of what it unearths is eye-poppingly surprising, the writers' cool scholarly approach means that the book never becomes preachy or prudish. Throughout, there is a wry humour: Theo Tait's essay on "How *Viz* made Britain ruder" had me laughing out loud. I'd recommend this book to anyone interested in Britain's uniquely yobbish and concomitantly dynamic culture.'
Francis Gilbert, author of *Yob Nation*

Once characterized as a polite nation, reserved and well-mannered, the British are increasingly seen as rude: a country of foul-mouthed football hooligans and drunken ladettes. *Rude Britannia* places these contemporary concerns about rudeness in relation to wider discussions of culture, class and national identity. Examining representations of rudeness in newspapers and the broadcast media, as well as in dictionaries, literature and popular culture, *Rude Britannia* contributes to current debates about the nature of Britishness.

Edited by Mina Gorji and featuring contributions from Tom Paulin, Deborah Cameron and Lynda Mugglestone, this timely and authoritative exploration of rudeness in modern English will be invaluable to those interested in the English language and British culture.

Mina Gorji is a Research Fellow at Magdalen College, Oxford University, where her research interests include literary language and eighteenth- and nineteenth-century literature. She is the author of the forthcoming title *John Clare and the Nature of Poetry*.

Rude Britannia

Edited by Mina Gorji

Routledge
Taylor & Francis Group

LONDON AND NEW YORK

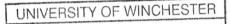
First published 2007
by Routledge
2 Park Square, Milton Park, Abingdon, Oxon OX14 4RN

Simultaneously published in the USA and Canada
by Routledge
270 Madison Ave, New York, NY 10016

*Routledge is an imprint of the Taylor & Francis Group, an informa
business*

© 2007 Mina Gorji

Typeset in Sabon by
RefineCatch Limited, Bungay, Suffolk
Printed and bound in Great Britain by
The Cromwell Press, Trowbridge, Wiltshire

British Library Cataloguing in Publication Data
A catalogue record for this book is available from the British Library

Library of Congress Cataloging-in-Publication Data
Rude Britannia / edited by Mina Gorji.
    p. cm.
1. Great Britain – Social life and customs – 20th century. 2. Great
Britain – Social life and customs – 21st century. 3. Conduct of life –
History – 20th century. 4. Conduct of life – History – 21st century.
5. Discourse analysis – Social aspects – Great Britain. 6. National
characteristics, British – History – 20th century. 7. National
characteristics, British – History – 21st century. I. Gorji, Mina,
1975–
    DA589.4.R83 2007
    395.0941 – dc22   2007003287

ISBN10: 0–415–38277–7 (pbk)
ISBN10: 0–415–38276–9 (hbk)

ISBN13: 978–0–415–38277–9 (pbk)
ISBN13: 978–0–415–38276–2 (hbk)

Contents

List of illustrations   vii
Notes on contributors   ix
Acknowledgements   xi

1   Introduction: Rude Britannia?   I
    MINA GORJI

PART I
The vulgar tongue   21

2   'The indefinable something': representing rudeness in the
    English dictionary   23
    LYNDA MUGGLESTONE

3   Poubellication: in the lexical dunny with the furphy king from
    down under   35
    VALENTINE CUNNINGHAM

4   Rude words   56
    TOM PAULIN

PART II
British bawdy   69

5   Orwell's dirty postcards   71
    DAVID PASCOE

6   How *Viz* made Britain ruder   82
     THEO TAIT

7   Bosom of the nation: Page Three in the 1970s and 1980s   96
     REBECCA LONCRAINE

PART III
The limits of rudeness   113

8   When Saturday comes: the boundaries of football rudeness   115
     TONY CROWLEY

9   Redefining rudeness: from polite social intercourse to
     'good communication'   127
     DEBORAH CAMERON

     Index   139

List of illustrations

Figures

1.1	Rude Britannia	1
1.2	Vicky Pollard	4
1.3	*Viz* Fat Slags	5
5.1	Postcard by McGill, c. 1940	72
5.2	Postcard by McGill, c. 1950	75
6.1	Johnny Fartpants	85
6.2	Sweary Mary	87
6.3	Rude Kid	88
6.4	*Viz* anthology front cover in the style of a Lad Mag cover	94
7.1	*Sun* cartoon	109

Table

9.1	Changing norms for social interaction	131

Notes on contributors

Deborah Cameron is a sociolinguist, and currently holds the Rupert Murdoch Chair of Language and Communication at the University of Oxford. She is the author of two books on changing norms and standards for communication, *Verbal Hygiene* (1995) and *Good to Talk?* (2000), and her most recent book is *On Language and Sexual Politics* (2006).

Tony Crowley is the Hartley Burr Alexander Chair in the Humanities at Scripps College, California, and Honorary Research Fellow in the Institute of Irish Studies at the University of Liverpool. He has published widely in the field of language and cultural theory, including *Standard English and the Politics of Language* (2003) and *Wars of Words: The Politics of Language in Ireland 1537–2004* (2005).

Valentine Cunningham is Professor of English Language and Literature at Oxford University, and Tutor and Fellow in English Literature at Corpus Christi College, Oxford. He reviews widely for journals and newspapers, and broadcasts regularly for BBC Radio on literary and musicological topics. He has published extensively on Victorian and Modern Literature, and his most recent book is *Reading After Theory* (2002).

Mina Gorji is a Research Fellow at Magdalen College, Oxford. She has published on eighteenth- and nineteenth-century literature, poetic awkwardness, labouring-class poetry and savage culture. She is author of the forthcoming title *John Clare and the Nature of Poetry*.

Rebecca Loncraine researched the history of Page Three as Vera Douie Fellow at the Women's Library in London. She is writing a biography of L. Frank Baum, author of *The Wizard of Oz*, for Penguin USA.

Lynda Mugglestone is Professor of the History of English at the University of Oxford, and a Fellow in English Language and Literature at Pembroke College. She broadcasts regularly on radio and television and has published widely on language in the late eighteenth and nineteenth centuries. Recent work includes *Lexicography and the OED: Pioneers in the Untrodden Forest*

(Oxford University Press, 2002), *'Talking Proper': The Rise of Accent as Social Symbol* (2nd edn, Oxford University Press, 2003), *Lost for Words: The Hidden History of the Oxford English Dictionary* (Yale University Press, 2004) and the recently published *The Oxford History of the English Language*.

David Pascoe is Reader in English at the University of Glasgow, and works principally on the relations between literature and culture in the nineteenth and twentieth centuries. He has edited Dickens and Thackeray and has published monographs on Peter Greenaway, on the semiotics of airports, and the cultural history of aircraft.

Tom Paulin is GM Young fellow in English at Hertford College, Oxford, and is a well-known poet and critic who appears regularly on television and radio. His most recent collection of poems is a work of translation called *The Road to Inver*. He has edited the *Faber Book of Vernacular Verse* (1990), published definitive critical studies of Hardy and Hazlitt, as well as several important collections of essays including *Minotaur* (1992) and *Crusoe's Secret* (1996); his latest collection of essays, *The Secret Life of Poems*, will be published next year.

Theo Tait is a journalist and literary critic and contributes to the *London Review of Books* and *Times Literary Supplement*.

Acknowledgements

I would like to thank the fellows of Magdalen College for electing me to a Research Fellowship, without which I would have been unable to complete this book. I would also like to thank *Viz* magazine for generously providing images free of charge, *News International* for providing financial support, Kirstin at Time Shift Productions, and Louisa Semelyn and Ursula Mallows at Routledge for their patience and encouragement.

I am grateful to Christopher Whalen who was a tireless, meticulous and humorous research assistant. For their advice and suggestions about the book at various stages, and for lively discussion I would like to thank: Luisa Calé, Deborah Cameron, Amit Chaudhuri, Tony Crowley, Jane Garnett, Rebecca Loncraine, Lynda Mugglestone, Bernard O'Donoghue, Tom Paulin, Luke Robinson and Fiona Stafford. Thanks also to my family for their enthusiasms and encouragement, and especially to my parents Naheed and Taghi Gorji, and my sisters, Ladan and Sousan Gorji.

Chapter 1

Introduction

Rude Britannia?

Mina Gorji

In 'Rude Britannia: A Nation Transformed', a cartoon published in the *Telegraph* on 29 August 2000 and reproduced in Figure 1.1, two icons sit side by side. The familiar image of Britannia, representative of civility and authority, looks over, shocked, at the figure on her right who is giving her the finger (a slang phrase which originated in the USA to describe the 'gesture with the middle finger raised . . . an obscene sign of contempt', *OED*). The cartoon depicts an anxiety which has been the subject of recent media debate: that traditional British reticence and restraint have given way to rudeness. This book places contemporary concerns about rudeness in relation to wider discussions of class, culture and national identity. Examining representations of rudeness in

Figure 1.1 Rude Britannia, by Steve Fricker.

newspapers and the broadcast media, as well as in dictionaries, literature and popular culture, it contributes to current debates about the nature of British-ness. It argues that rudeness is more than just offence: it has a cultural history.

A number of recent articles have voiced concern that Britain is growing ruder: for example, Yasmin Alibhai-Brown, writing in the *Independent* in 2003, criticized rising levels of incivility and bad behaviour (Alibhai-Brown 2003: 15). The phrase 'Rude Britannia' has become something of a popular headline over the last few years, appearing in the *Express* (20 June 2006), the *Daily Mail* (15 June 2005), the *Mirror* (4 November 2003) and the *Independent* (15 February 1998). 'Rude Britannia' is also the title of an article published in *Prospect* magazine in May 2001 in which Michael Elliot, editor of the *Economist* and *Newsweek International*, describes a revolution in the manners of the nation:

> Britain has become a society whose standards of civility seem to have collapsed and where much public behaviour has become astonishingly coarse – a place where aggression, vulgarity and drunkenness are com-monplace. . . . The sense that incivility has become a distinct social problem is growing.
>
> (Elliott 2001)

He ascribes this 'collapse' to a decline in class-based deference to figures of authority and their values, which is, he argues, the result of a complex set of social and economic changes: the end of Empire, the rise of the welfare state, the emergence of the 'permissive society' and consumer capitalism.

Addressing parliament on 19 July 2004 in a speech designed to coincide with the launch of the Home Office's five-year plan for tackling crime, Tony Blair blamed the permissive culture of the 'swinging sixties' for rising crime, social breakdown, vandalism, widening social inequalities and what he termed 'the loss of civility' in Britain. Recent government legislation, such as the introduction of Anti-Social Behaviour Orders (ASBOs), the public security measures in the Crime and Disorder Act of 1998 and the home secretary Jack Straw's determination to address drink-related crime suggest that incivility continues to be considered a target of social policy. Another response to the perceived rise in British 'rudeness' has been the proliferation, and popularity, of conduct literature over the last few years, including Lynne Truss's *Talk to the Hand: The Utter Bloody Rudeness of Everyday Life (Or Six Good Reasons to Stay Home and Bolt the Door)*, Simon Fanshawe's *The Done Thing: Negotiating the Minefield of Modern Manners*, Thomas Blaikie's *Guide to Modern Manners*, and Laurence and Jacqueline Llewelyn-Bowen's *A Pinch of Posh: A Beginner's Guide to Being Civilised*. Truss mourns 'the apparent collapse of civility in all areas of our dealing with strangers' (2005: 2–3) and argues that this decline can partly be explained by social changes – 'adherence to "manners" has broken down just as money and celebrity have largely replaced birth as the measure of social status' (12).

But although we may no longer 'equate posh behaviour with good behaviour' (Truss 2005: 7), rudeness is still often viewed as a sign of low social status. This association is registered in the history of the word itself: although the dominant contemporary sense of 'rude' describes behaviour or language which causes offence, in the eighteenth and nineteenth centuries the word was also used as a term of social description: 'Uneducated, unlearned; ignorant; lacking in knowledge or book-learning' (*OED* 1a), and 'Devoid of, or deficient in, culture or refinement; uncultured, unrefined' (3a). Because 'book-learning' and 'refinement' tended to be associated with the well-off and socially privileged minority, those described as 'rude' (in these senses) were likely to be poor and of low social rank. Although the use of rude language and behaviour is not confined to a particular social group, nonetheless rudeness is still imaged in terms of low class.

The cartoon image of Rude Britannia plays with this prevailing stereotype: her physical appearance as well as the offensive gesture she is making are signs of being 'common'. Rather than the traditional Corinthian helmet, she wears a baseball cap; instead of modest, formal robes, she is squeezed into a tight dress, breasts bulging out, teamed with a pair of tracksuit trousers and trainers, the uniform of a 'chav' (a derogatory slang term used to describe 'a young person of a type characterized by brash and loutish behaviour and the wearing of designer-style clothes (esp. sportswear); usually with connotations of a low social status', *OED Online* draft entry, June 2006). She is also noticeably fatter than her predecessor, and being overweight is another stereotypical indicator of low social status.

Historically, middle-class values have been expressed and enforced through control of the female body and regulation of desire. In the collection of essays *The Ideology of Conduct* (1987), Nancy Armstrong and Leonard Tennenhouse discuss how notions of respectability and modesty were constructed as middle-class values in conduct literature (from the middle ages to the present day); instructional literature both recorded but also helped to produce a middle-class ideology about women and desire which exerted discursive control over the public sphere. Considered in this context, Rude Britannia's relaxed posture and unkempt, slatternly appearance transgress these middle-class norms and mark her humble social rank; she is a slob and a yob. No lady, she resembles Vicky Pollard from *Little Britain* (Figure 1.2), or one of *Viz* magazine's Fat Slags (Figure 1.3). Like them, she might be described as a 'ladette', 'A young woman characterized by her enjoyment of social drinking, sport, or other activities typically considered to be male-oriented, and often by attitudes or behaviour regarded as irresponsible or brash' (*OED Online* draft entry, June 2001). A beer can sits crumpled by her feet and she is smoking a cigarette, a habit increasingly perceived as anti-social. She has appropriated and transformed the symbolic language which governs British national identity.

The butch, beer-drinking, and corpulent Britannia evokes another icon of national identity: John Bull. Invented in 1712, this plump and plain-speaking

Figure 1.2 Vicky Pollard.

embodiment of British rudeness became a stock figure in caricature of the period (see Hunt 2003). But 'Rude Britannia' also calls up other eighteenth-century iconographies. The structure of the cartoon itself recalls Rowlandson's popular caricature, 'The Contrast' (1792) (Franklin *et al.* 2003: 26). Here too the familiar image of Britannia sits on the left; a stern version of Pallas Athene, helmeted and draped in robes, she represents a polite icon threatened by change. Associated with naval power and commercial strength, she symbolizes a polite and commercial people. Yet her origins were not polite: in English iconography she dates back to the seventeenth century. After the return of Charles II, her image was stamped on to coins in 1672. But this image of authority became associated with the King's licentiousness, since it was believed that the model used was the royal mistress, the Duchess of Richmond, Frances Stewart. Noticing the likeness, Samuel Pepys remarked, 'a pretty

Figure 1.3 Viz Fat Slags.

thing it is that he should choose her face to represent Britannia by' (Warner 1996: 45).

In the eighteenth century, Britannia gained currency as a symbol of the freedom of the constitution. An icon of a libertarian opposition to established authority, she represented the freedoms enjoyed by the British rather than the authority vested in their rulers (Warner 1996: 47). She often appeared in eighteenth-century caricatures as a threatened woman, rather than as an armed Athena (Dickinson 1986: 52–3, 82–3; Hunt 2003: 121–69). Gillray's 1793 cartoon 'Fashion before Ease', for example, shows Tom Paine bracing himself against Britannia's bottom and trying to force her into a tight-fitting French corset (Dickinson 1986: 144–5). Here, Britannia appears as a buxom wench, an alternative image of English liberty, resisting attempts to contain her body and control her freedoms (see Dresser 1989). But the idea of the nation as a maiden offered an ambiguous representation of conflicting notions of liberty. It is as an embodiment of British liberties that she returns in the image of a polite maiden to contrast with the dishevelled, Medusa-like figure of disreputable French liberty in Rowlandson's 'The Contrast' (1792). These two contrasting iconographies come together in the 2004 cartoon: Britannia the polite maiden is now placed in 1960, whereas Rude Britannia with her ample cleavage recalls her blowsy, libertarian ancestor.

Britannia was a personification of the nation and the freedoms of the constitution, but she also came to represent the might and authority of the British

Empire. The phrase 'Rude Britannia' alludes to James Thomson's well-known patriotic ode of 1740, 'Rule Britannia', which was set to music by Thomas Augustine Arne and became an unofficial national anthem and hymn to Empire:

> Rule, Britannia! Britannia, rule the waves:
> Britons never will be slaves.

Where Britannia symbolizes liberty, Rude Britannia appears to be taking liberties. Where Britannia embodies imperial rule, Rude Britannia breaks the rules. Britannia was a symbol of civil values: rudeness was not part of her official iconography, but associated with her colonial subjects. And yet although Britannia is supposed to represent civility, propriety and decency, Empire was rude in the most brutal sense.

Labelling certain people as rude and others as civilized was one way in which Empire exerted a form of control and authority over its subjects. In *Considerations on Representative Government*, published in 1861, John Stuart Mill used the words 'rude', 'uncivilized', 'primitive' and 'savage' to describe those 'inferior' races colonized by Britain. In his writing, being rude or civilized are essential values associated with particular ethnic groups. Such 'rude' people, Mill argued, could not enjoy the liberty and democracy he championed at home because they lacked the capacity to monitor and restrain their behaviour: 'A rude people, though in some degree alive to the benefits of civilized society, may be unable to practice the forbearance it demands' and so for 'any people who have emerged from savage life', only a 'limited and qualified freedom' would be appropriate (Mill 1958: 7; see Chaudhuri 2003: 210–13 for a discussion of Mill's use of the word 'rude'). Mill pleaded for political liberty and democratic governance, while attempting to justify their unsuitability for certain peoples. His condemnation of censorship was the basis for Bernard Williams's 1979 reform of legislation on obscenity and film censorship. But whilst Mill argued that forms of outrage and disturbance (those that did not cause harm) were to be welcomed and nurtured in a free society, such liberties were confined to 'civilized' nations and peoples.

Rude Britannia is shocking because she challenges a dominant association of Britannia with Empire and authority. The cartoon calls into question a prevailing model of British national identity and registers the 'cultural disorientation that accompanies the collapse of imperial certainties' (Gilroy 2004: 125). The devolution of British governance in the late 1990s has heightened this sense of post-imperial disorientation and prompted questions about national identity and the definition of Britishness.

The phrase 'Rude Britannia' alludes to Thomson's patriotic hymn to Empire, but it also calls up a competing history. Although the familiar Pallas Athene version of Britannia is an imperial icon for an imperial nation, Britannia was the Latin name given to England and Wales by the colonizing Romans. She was originally an allegory developed to characterize a conquered country. The word 'rude' itself has Roman roots, deriving from the Latin word *rudis*, and carries the sense of 'unwrought, unformed, inexperienced'. In early Roman iconography Britannia was represented as rude in the sense of 'primitive' and 'savage'. One early image, a carving from Aphrodisias in Asia Minor, shows Britannia as a captive, dragged by the hair by emperor Claudius, with her right breast bared like an Amazon: here she is 'rude' in the sense of 'uncivilized' and 'barbarous' (*OED* 3b). She also appeared on early Roman coins looking fierce and warlike, wearing spiked armour – 'rude' in the sense of 'violent, harsh' (*OED* 5). Although Britannia became a symbol of civility and imperial rule, in early representations she was depicted as a 'savage' colonial subject. The figure of Imperial Britannia, often represented in armour and armed with a trident has transformed this into a form of 'civilized' rudeness. Rude Britannia subverts this image of imperial authority but she also calls up her 'uncivilized' original.

Rude language

The Rude Britannia cartoon depicts 1960 as a watershed in the history of British identity, the end of the polite nation. This was the year of the Lady Chatterley trial, a key moment in the history of rudeness. First published in Italy in 1928, the uncensored version of the book was banned in Britain until 1960. Both the language and the subject of the novel, the affair between Lady Chatterley and her gamekeeper Oliver Mellors, the son of a miner, were perceived as obscene and as socially and morally subversive. In response to the Obscene Publications Act of 1959, Penguin Books defended, and won the right to publish, certain words and sexually explicit scenes which had been expurgated from earlier editions of Lawrence's novel. Bookshops all over England sold out of Penguin's first run of the novel – a total of 200,000 copies – on the first day of publication. Within a year, the book had sold two million copies.

The trial was a landmark in the story of English literature, but it also came to mark a moment of cultural transition, ushering in a decade associated with the new permissive society (the *OED*'s first citation of this phrase dates from 1956). Philip Larkin's poem 'Annus Mirabilis' begins with a reference to the trial:

> Sexual intercourse began
> In nineteen sixty-three
> (Which was rather late for me) –
> Between the end of the *Chatterley* ban
> And the Beatles' first LP.
> (Larkin 1988: 161)

The novel's explicit scenes and use of taboo language, its description of *fucking* rather than the more technical and circumspect 'sexual intercourse', caused controversy. The words *fuck* and *cunt* provided a focus for wider discussion about social change and the emergence of what was referred to as 'the permissive society'.

During the Chatterley trial, the counsel for the prosecution, Mervyn Griffith-Jones, attacked the book's obscenities: 'The word "fuck" or "fucking" occurs no less than thirty times; "shit" and "arse" six times apiece; "cock" four times; "piss" three times, and so on' (Rolph 1961: 20). He famously asked the jury: 'Is it a book that you would even wish your wife or your servants to read?' (17). Griffith-Jones's comments register a male ideology of shielding women from obscenity and a paternalism that sought to protect servants from corruption. The trial was not just about obscenity, it became symbolic of more sweeping changes in the class structure of British society; it offers one concentrated example of how the discussion of rude language can gather to itself questions about moral values and social symbolic power. The boundaries of rudeness are not fixed but socially and historically determined. Debates about rudeness often mark struggles for cultural authority which erupt at particular points of crisis or social change.

Lawrence himself had been trying to redeem these 'four-letter words' from vulgar and obscene associations. One of the ways in which he attempted to do this was by 'turn[ing] on the dialect', which was, according to F. R. Leavis, 'a way of putting over the "four-letter words" ' – of trying to reclaim them as non-obscene (Coombes 1973: 417, 416). The following scene was available to British readers for the first time in the 1960 edition:

> 'Tha'rt good cunt, though, aren't ter? Best bit o' cunt left on earth. When ter likes! When tha'rt willin'!'
> 'What is cunt?' she said.
> 'An' doesn't ter know? Cunt! It's thee down theer; an' what I get when I'm i'side thee, and what tha gets when I'm i'side thee; it's a' as it is, all on't.'
> 'All on't,' she teased. 'Cunt! It's like fuck then.'
> 'Nay nay! Fuck's only what you do. Animals fuck. But cunt's a lot more than that. It's thee, dost see: an' tha'rt a lot besides an animal, aren't ter? – even ter fuck? Cunt! Eh, that's the beauty o' thee, lass!'
>
> (Lawrence 1960: 185)

In this extract, two kinds of rude or 'deviant' language are associated: dialect and obscenity. This scene represents a moment of social subversion both in the sense of challenging the norms of polite conversation, but also because by defining the word *cunt* to Lady Chatterley, Mellors is demonstrating authority over his social superior.

Allowing obscene words into print was perceived by some contemporaries as a gesture of class defiance, a victory over prudish middle-class values. In the words of 'Beluncle', writing in the *New Statesman* on 12 November 1960, the trial was a 'triumph for a working-class writer [i.e. D. H. Lawrence]'. He went on to quote a taxi-driver's comments about the trial: ' "What they will have to do now," said the taxi-driver on my return, "is to put all those four-letter words in the dictionary" ' (cited in Burchfield 1972). The publication of the novel in 1960 led to a lively public discussion about the desirability of including what had been long-banned sexual taboo words in dictionaries.

By 1969, the words *fuck* and *cunt* were included in the *Penguin English Dictionary* (1965) and the *American Heritage Dictionary* (1969). Although *cunt* appeared in *Webster's Third New International Dictionary* (1971), the word *fuck* was dropped at galley-proof stage. It was to be 12 years before these words were included in the *Shorter Oxford English Dictionary*. The editors of the satirical 1960s magazine *OZ* wrote to the delegates of OUP in April 1969 asking for explanation as to why the word *fuck* had been excluded. Replying on behalf of delegates of the press, Dan Davin explained that although four-letter words had been included in dictionaries of slang, what he termed 'serious' and 'general' dictionaries had excluded these words. He recognized a change in the climate of popular opinion:

> the permissive attitudes that now prevail are of such recent date that they have not yet had time to become reflected in large dictionaries that can only be revised and reset at fairly long intervals for reasons of cost. And to have included the four-letter words, until recently, in dictionaries meant for general use might have meant their being banned in this country and elsewhere.
>
> (cited in Burchfield 1972)

Even in January 1968, a year before this letter, the delegates had approved the principle of including *cunt* and *fuck* in the new *Supplement* to the *OED* in recognition of the fact that 'standards of tolerance have changed and their omission has for many years, and more frequently of late, excited critical comment' (unpublished letter of 5 January 1968, cited in Burchfield 1972). The words appeared in the new supplement in 1972.

Although the 1960s saw 'a radical change in the freedom of language and sexuality depicted in publications and public entertainment' (Hughes 1998: 194), even in this so-called permissive age there was resistance and disagreement as to the appropriate limits of these freedoms. *Fuck* became the subject of debate once again in 1965, after the theatre critic Kenneth Tynan became the first person to use the word on television during a live debate, aired as part of the BBC's satirical show *BBC3* broadcast on 13 November. Discussing the subject of censorship, Tynan explained, 'I doubt if there are very many rational people in this world to whom the word "fuck" is particularly diabolical or revolting or totally forbidden' (cited in Hughes 1998: 195). This was the first time the word had been heard on British television. It caused a public outcry, which prompted a formal apology by the BBC and four House of Commons motions which were signed by 133 Labour and Tory backbenchers. In December

1976, Sex Pistol 'Johnny Rotten' used the word *fuck* on an early evening live television show, provoking public outrage: the Sex Pistols were blacklisted from television, the show's presenter was suspended, and the programme was taken off the air a few months later.

In the decades since this outburst, there seems to have been a change of attitude to the use of rude language on television. According to the findings of a report commissioned by the Institute of Communication Studies for the Broadcasting Standards Commission, 1997, 'Regulating for Changing Values', there has been an increase in the use of words which were previously considered to be taboo in public broadcasting. Some participants felt that the proliferation of such language 'indicated a decline in social standards and was seen as a sign of unsociable behaviour' (cited in Hargrave 2000: 5). The pervasiveness of rude language in public culture was perceived as a sign of the nation's declining moral and social health, and of a decline in respect for authority.

More recently still, in 2005, the public communications regulator, the Office of Communications (usually known as Ofcom), conducted a public survey of attitudes to swearing and offensive language. All participants felt that 'swearing' and the use of 'strong language' had become 'endemic in society', not only on television, but also 'in public places, schools, on the street and in some workplaces' (Ofcom 2005: 10). This increase was seen by some of the participants as 'a symptom of a decline in public standards' (2).

In February 2004 John Lydon – the former Johnny Rotten – appeared live on the television show *I'm a Celebrity Get Me Out of Here!* and described viewers as 'fucking cunts' for failing to choose him as the show's loser; but compared with the outrage his swearing had caused in the 1970s, his expletive outburst caused barely a stir: it riled only a handful of the programme's 11 million viewers, provoking fewer than 100 complaints two days after the incident. When selected members of the viewing public were shown the Lydon clip as part of the Ofcom survey into attitudes to swearing and offensive language in 2005, they did not rate it as 'highly offensive' in part because it was the sort of language they expected from this particular celebrity, but also because the outburst occurred at around 10.28pm, well after the 9pm watershed, after which programmes thought to be unsuitable for children would be shown (Ofcom 2005: 36–7). Since it did not occur on a family viewing programme, this language was not seen to be as offensive as it might have been had it occurred in a different context.

But what some have perceived as an apparent increase in the use of rude language in public discourse registers a category shift rather than a quantitative increase in rudeness. The boundaries of rudeness have shifted. The conventions which govern the use of 'rude' language in public discourse have altered over the last generation. Although the word *fuck* is still censored in certain newspapers, written as f***, and bleeped in some broadcast television and radio programmes, in many contexts it is markedly less offensive than it was in the 1960s. In certain situations, especially in informal conversation, it can be used now as an intensifier, or else as a marker of strong feelings.

The use of rude insults by politicians is another example of a shift in attitudes to rude language: although in the past leaders and ministers may well have used such language in private conversation, it is unlikely that this would have been reported by the leading newspapers and media outlets of the day in, say, the 1950s (see Chapter 8). Nonetheless, a lack of clear consensus about lines of taboo and norms of acceptability continues to prompt debate.

Another area of significant change in attitudes to rude language has been a shift in perceptions of religious terms of abuse. A survey by the Broadcasting Standards Commission (part of the Broadcasting Standards Council set up to monitor taste and decency) carried out in 1998 found that although words such as *cunt*, *motherfucker* and *fuck* have remained strongly offensive in certain contexts, religious words such as *Christ*, *God*, *bloody* and *damn* had become weaker (Hargrave 1998: 49). However, in the years since this report, religion has become a subject of sensitivity and renewed debate in the wake of government legislation criminalizing expressions of religious hatred and intolerance.

In a survey of attitudes to the use of offensive language in broadcasting, conducted in 2000 by the Advertising Standards Authority, British Broadcasting Corporation, Broadcasting Standards Commission and the Independent Television Commission, participants were asked to rank offensive words in order of severity: racial abuse, such as *Paki* and *nigger*, was at the top of the scale, and such terms were 'felt to be unacceptable in today's society' (Hargrave 2000: 7–8). Many now consider terms such as *nigger* and *Paki* as more strongly offensive than those terms describing genitalia or sexual behaviour such as *slut* or *tart*. (For discussions of changing lines of taboo see Sierz 2001; Hughes 1998: 184–235; and Andersson and Trudgill 1990: 35–66.) In 2004, for example, the football commentator Ron Atkinson was forced to resign after he described Marcel Desailly, the Chelsea captain, as a 'fucking lazy thick nigger', during a television broadcast. In the 1960s, linguistic impropriety might have caused more outrage than racist language, and the word *fucking* deemed more offensive than *nigger*. But there has been a change in the structure of feeling associated with race and racism in British society, and although some argue that terms such as *Paki* and *nigger* are acceptable when they are 'taken back' by groups who were once the target of the words, such language is, in general usage, no longer tolerated.

Raymond Williams argued that the history of a language registered changes in structures of feeling, which he defined as 'meanings and values as they are actively lived and felt' (Williams 1977: 132). Not only semantic shifts but also changing attitudes to the use and definition of what constitutes 'rude' language reflect and refract wider social transformations in complex ways. If words formerly considered taboo are now licensed in public, does that imply that the way we configure the public sphere, as well as the way in which we define taboo, has changed?

Rude language and class

Responding to an article in the *Financial Times* 'Here's to the New Prudes' (2004a), one angry reader condemned the proliferation of 'four-letter words' on television, explaining that 'it used to be that only builder's labourers with limited education interspersed the "f" word as every other word in their speech. Now it appears to be de rigueur for every chat show host' (2004b). As well as registering disapproval, his comment also suggests an anxiety that social distinctions are becoming blurred; this is based on a stereotypical imaging of rudeness in terms of class. This association of the use of rude language with low social status is both described (and confirmed) by the social anthropologist Gillian Evans in her 2006 study of a white working-class 'tribe' in Bermondsey, *Educational Failure and White Working Class Children in Britain*. Evans interviewed one of the residents, Sharon (a name which itself emblematizes a particular social stereotype: 'A disparaging name for females considered to be working class, unintelligent and vulgarly dressed, generally below the social standards acceptable to the user of the phrase' (<http://www.peevish.co.uk/slang/s.htm> accessed December 2006). Sharon defined herself as 'common':

> When I ask Sharon what being common means, she tells me: 'Bein' common is about bein' down to earth, not f[th]inkin' you're upper [better than other people]; it means tellin' it like it is, and it means ya don't mind yer Ps 'n' Qs: ya don't try to talk proper.' In Sharon's home, being common means that swearing (foul language) – shit, fuck, bastard, fucking, fucking-hell and cunt – is a familiar part of everyday speech. . . . Having none of the obsessive modesty of prudish politeness, Sharon revels in the permanent joke of the body's sexual and excretory functions and she makes no attempt to conceal them for the sake of civility. Without a doubt, being common is, for Sharon, about a particular relationship to the question of what counts in polite society as good manners and it is a relationship of opposition.
>
> (Evans 2006: 23–4)

Sharon's use of rude language – swear words and references to taboo bodily functions – marks her as 'common'. In this extract, Evans distinguishes her own (higher) social position from Sharon's by her use of language. She studiously avoids the eschatological register: the phrase 'the body's sexual and excretory functions' is technical, Latinate, and vague, and thus it sidesteps the blunt, corporeal rudeness it describes. Evans uses Standard English to represent her own 'polite' speech whilst using the non-standard code of writing to represent Sharon's talk, who uses *bein'* rather than *being*, *ya* instead of *you*. In this extract, both *ya* and *bein'* are themselves coded images of class associated with deviancy. (For a discussion of the relationship between social class and linguistic propriety see Mugglestone 2003.) This extract shows very clearly how stereotypes of linguistic rudeness and politeness can function as class indicators. The categorizing and recognition of certain social practices – forms of behaviour, language and cultural objects – as rude and others as polite is one way of maintaining specific forms of political and cultural authority and symbolic power.

Like *barbarism* and *civilization, polite* and *rude* are complex evaluative words which figure prominently in the current debate and metadiscourse, but they are not stable terms. In academic discussion, *politeness* has been defined and discussed by linguists and social scientists such as Lakoff (1973), Leech (1983), Brown and Levinson (1987) and Watts (2003) as that behaviour which allows the avoidance of hostile confrontation, and rudeness as behaviour which is unfriendly and causes hostile confrontation, including the use of offensive, emotional or vitriolic language. But although there is some consensus about how to define rude language in linguistic discourse, the question of how to evaluate rude language is open to debate.

Although recent commentators have been critical of the perceived increase in bad language, viewing it as a sign of moral decline, Lakoff has suggested that rising levels of linguistic rudeness, known as verbal 'coarsening', might be interpreted as a positive sign of democracy. She has described verbal incivility as a mark of positive sociological change, both a sign and a result of the enfranchisement of previously marginalized social groups. An increase in rudeness, then, marks a moment of cultural transition, registering a shift in the social structure whereby previously disenfranchised social groups gain political power:

> Geniality and consensus tend to flourish in societies that are homogenous and in which all members share common interests; or, failing that, where only one group, itself homogenous, has the ability or right to control public discourse. . . . what is taken by many as a decline in civility actually represents an increase in democracy, and the enrichment of public discourse with radically new opinions, daringly expressed.
>
> (Lakoff 2003: 41, 43)

Rising levels of rudeness mark moments of social transition. Rather than representing the collapse of civil society, Rude Britannia might be a sign of democracy in rude health.

Rude culture/polite society

Contemporary ideas of rudeness and politeness are not essential but historically formed. Since the eighteenth century, the values of politeness have shaped and controlled public discourse. The German philosopher Jürgen Habermas describes these changes in sociological and historical terms. He argues that in the eighteenth century an emerging class created for itself a cultural, social and linguistic identity. One of the discursive practices through which this social identity was defined was politeness. Politeness in the eighteenth century was the hallmark of the gentry and represented values which became, according to the linguist Richard J. Watts, 'the socially desirable goal for the new upwardly mobile middle classes of society' (Watts 2003: 34). In the eighteenth century, politeness was part of an 'ideological discourse through which the British social class system came into being' (35) and systems of politeness are still 'part of a discourse that discriminates against and excludes large groups of the population from highly valued symbolic and material resources' (42).

Politeness referred to more than manners or social behaviour; it was a language of social and cultural description and evaluation, according to which the gentlemanly was considered to be normative over a wide range of expressive forms. The vocabulary of polite behaviour was replicated in discussion of the arts and learning. Politeness set up reciprocal relations between elite social status and cultural expression: the term referred to a range of other discourses which make up what we tend to call 'culture' today, namely 'polite learning', 'polite arts' and 'polite letters' (see Klein 1984, 1986; Langford 1989: 71). But although politeness emerged as a dominant discourse in the eighteenth century, it did not dominate public behaviour or public culture, as Vic Gatrell's recent study of sex and satire in eighteenth-century London reveals (Gatrell 2006).

Nonetheless, the production and enforcement of forms of politeness as a norm created and maintained forms of cultural authority, and shaped definitions of national identity. The description of the British as a 'polite and commercial people' was coined in the eighteenth century, and politeness is still perceived by some as a defining feature of national identity. Being 'polite' is first on the list of characteristics Jeremy Paxman identifies with the English:

> Once upon a time the English knew who they were. There was such a ready list of adjectives to hand. They were polite, unexcitable, reserved and had hot-water bottles instead of a sex life. . . . They were class-bound, hidebound and incapable of expressing their emotions.
>
> (Paxman 1998: 1)

Yet there are other constructions of national identity which do not depend on politeness: national identity need not only be defined according to the norms of a particular (privileged) social group. In the eighteenth century, for example, the figure of John Bull challenged the polite nation. This corpulent, beer-drinking, plain-speaking archetype of rude Englishness was often contrasted with the apparently effeminate, polite and sophisticated Frenchman.

The discourse of politeness is one example of how social and behavioural norms have shaped and defined linguistic and cultural practice. The discourse of manners has shaped the language we use to discuss culture and national identity. Like politeness, the term 'rude' can be used to describe language and culture as well as behaviour. One of the senses of 'rude' recorded in the *OED* is 'Devoid of, or deficient in, culture or refinement'; but culture need not be refined, or defined in terms of politeness. Rude language, culture and behaviours are not always deliberately subversive of polite rules, but often draw on norms with their own history and legitimacy.

The essays in this volume present rudeness as a locus for struggles over social and cultural value. They investigate some of the forms and the force of rudeness in modern Britain, mapping out a number of different cultural and linguistic contexts in which rudeness is expressed, evaluated and discussed – on television, in literature, dictionaries, the tabloids, football chants, magazines, self-help books and seaside postcards. They show that rudeness in popular culture is as much about a deliberate attempt to push the barriers of censorship and debunk the self-appointed elite of taste as it is about being uncivil.

The book is divided into three parts in order to draw out common questions and themes. The essays in Part I, 'The vulgar tongue', consider definitions of and attitudes to rude words in dictionaries. The category of rude words does not only include taboo words or expletives but other terms which did not form part of the vocabulary of polite conversation including slang and dialect.

Lynda Mugglestone considers how early lexicographers handled rude words. Her essay examines the complexities (social, linguistic, and cultural) which have often attended the representation of rude words within the English dictionary. She explores the uses of politeness in the lexicographical representation of words which infringed on the cultural norms of the polite world, both in the principles and the practice of the *OED*.

Valentine Cunningham describes another kind of vulgar lexicography: slang dictionaries. He looks at the language of the social, geographical, moral and lexicographical periphery, those words banished from polite English circles. His essay focuses on Eric Partridge, author of numerous dictionaries of the vulgar tongue, and describes his various attempts to give history and status to words which were considered rude by Partridge's contemporaries.

Tom Paulin turns his attention to other forms of rude language, focusing on the use of regional accent and dialect. He lists and discusses many of those intimate, familiar, uncouth Ulster words which have been excluded from the language of polite polished conversation, and, until recently, from dictionaries. Such words are not rude in the sense of bawdy or offensive, but carry a sense of their own uncouth quirky qualities, and are often able to express affection and an intimate quality unavailable in polite discourse. Paulin offers his own personal dictionary of the Ulster tongue. His list of familiar personal words opens up what might be seen as a secret, closed communication, making public a private word hoard: it is both a form of and comment on lexicography but also a prose poem of sorts.

A new sense of rude was recorded in 1961, meaning offensive with reference to sexual organs or functions; this sense, which is in common usage, was only added to the Additions Series of the *OED* in 1993. The three essays in Part II, 'British bawdy', consider the representation of taboo, sexuality and the body in popular culture, including tabloids, seaside postcards, comics and lad magazines. All three essays discuss how questions of taboo and obscenity work through and call into question social issues and values through the use of double entendre, euphemism and forms of licensed subversion.

David Pascoe analyses the seaside postcard, an icon of British rudeness, paying particular attention to the works of Donald McGill. He considers George Orwell's discussion of McGill's work as a form of protest against the obscenity of social inequality, suggesting McGill's art was far more effective than the impolite and patronizing illustrations of working-class life in northern England that he had published a few years earlier in *The Road to Wigan Pier* (1937).

Dubbed as the 'four-letter comic', *Viz* magazine became a national forum for lavatory humour, pushing into print and mass circulation a certain kind of private, schoolboy rudeness. Theo Tait considers how *Viz* has its own strict codes, arguing that there is fastidiousness, even a classical restraint about how it represents rudeness – naughtiness depends on its deft and delicate play with taboo.

In the last essay in this part, Rebecca Loncraine focuses on the issue of rudeness and gender. She describes the ways in which the *Sun*'s Page Three contributed to contemporary debates about nudity in public culture. She argues that Page Three was a space in which ideas of rudeness were both expressed, exploited and tested.

The essays in the final part, 'The limits of rudeness', consider the changing boundaries of rudeness in contemporary discourse. Tony Crowley considers the changing norms and rules for rudeness in football chants, arguing that it is a form of discourse which has clear conventions about what is acceptable and what is not. Football chants are often seen as rude, violent and without rules; but he explains that they have their own codes, rules and rituals. His essay is concerned with racial abuse and the way in which that has shifted both in football and more widely in British discourses. He argues that rude chanting can produce communal bonds and identities and analyses the relationship between class and rudeness, drawing out and developing a common theme which has been discussed in previous chapters.

Deborah Cameron describes and accounts for changing norms of polite discourse, arguing that ways of talking which were seen as rude are now considered polite. Recently, traditional British notions of 'polite' and 'rude' behaviour towards others have come under pressure from a new ideology of interpersonal communication, promoted by a new group of experts (therapists, management gurus, 'communication skills' trainers) and disseminated by a variety of institutions from businesses to the popular mass media. According to these new norms, the social distance and reticence traditionally associated with polite discourse is now considered rude. This apparent shift in values is the subject of Steven Frears's recent film *The Queen* (2006), which contrasts the Queen's formality and restraint in her public statements about the death of Diana with Prime Minister Blair's more emotional, direct response, which represents a new informal, emotional public language. Cameron examines the changing nature of 'expert' definitions of rude and polite interpersonal behaviour, and discusses the (not always positive) reception new ideas about 'good communication' have had in Britain.

The essays in this collection consider different ways in which rudeness has been described, managed, contained, skirted around, and expressed both verbally and visually. They chart its changing shapes, boundaries and values in modern British culture. Using a variety of contemporary and historical materials, they analyse the different ways in which rudeness has been defined and evaluated, uncovering the social relations of symbolic power which govern rudeness. Through a discussion of rude practices, the essays also explore ways in which ideas of class have shaped the way in which certain kinds of language and culture have been classified and evaluated. Common concerns include linguistic and social codes, standards of decency, the nature of taboo in the public realm, constructions of bawdy, class, definitions of popular culture, race, gender and British identity.

Whose values determine and shape public discourse? What can changing attitudes to and definitions of rudeness tell us? What is the place of rudeness in modern British culture: is it always confined to the provincial, colonial, and socio-economic margins? What forms can rudeness take? What kinds of social questions are symbolically at stake in discussions of rudeness? What is the relationship between the moral, social and linguistic aspects of rudeness? These are some of the questions raised by the essays in this collection. Together they explore and describe a cultural history of British rudeness.

References

Alibhai-Brown, Y. (2003) 'There Is No Excuse For All This Bad Behaviour', *Independent*, 22 September 2003, available online at <http://www.independent.co.uk/incoming/article87888.ece> (accessed December 2006).

Andersson, L. and Trudgill, P. (1990) *Bad Language*, Oxford: Blackwell.

Armstrong, N. and Tennenhouse, L. (1987) *The Ideology of Conduct: Essays on Literature and the History of Sexuality*, New York: Methuen.

Brown, P. and Levinson, S. C. (1987) *Politeness: Some Universals of Language Use*, Cambridge: Cambridge University Press.

Burchfield, R. W. (1972) 'Four-Letter Words and the *OED*', *TLS*, 13 October, p. 1233.

Chaudhuri, A. (2003) *D. H. Lawrence and 'Difference'*, Oxford: Clarendon Press.

Coombes, H. (ed.) (1973) *D. H. Lawrence: A Critical Anthology*, Harmondsworth: Penguin.

Dickinson, H. T. (1986) *Caricatures and the Constitution 1760–1832*, Cambridge: Chadwyck-Healey.

Dresser, M. (1989) 'Britannia', in R. Samuel (ed.) *Patriotism: The Making and*

Unmaking of British National Identity, London: Routledge, vol. 3: *National Fictions*, pp. 26–49.

Elliott, M. (2001) 'Rude Britannia', *Prospect* 63, May 2001, available online at <http://www.prospect-magazine.co.uk/article_details.php?id=3554> (accessed December 2006).

Evans, G. (2006) *Educational Failure and White Working Class Children in Britain*, Basingstoke: Palgrave Macmillan.

Financial Times (2004a) 'Here's to the New Prudes', *FT Weekend* October 2–3.

—— (2004b) Letters to the Editor, October 9, p. 12.

Franklin, A., Philp, M. and Navickas, K. (2003) *Napoleon and the Invasion of Britain*, Oxford: Bodleian Library.

Gatrell, V. (2006) *City of Laughter: Sex and Satire in Eighteenth-Century London*, London: Atlantic.

Gilroy, P. (2004) *After Empire: Melancholia or Convivial Culture?*, Abingdon: Routledge.

Hargrave, A. H. (1998) *Bad Language: What Are the Limits?*, London: Broadcasting Standards Commission.

—— (2000) *Delete Expletives?*, London: Broadcasting Standards Commission.

Hughes, G. (1998) *Swearing: A Social History of Foul Language, Oaths and Profanity in English*, London: Penguin.

Hunt, T. L. (2003) 'Britannia, John Bull and National Identity', in *Defining John Bull: Political Caricature and National Identity in Late Georgian England*, Aldershot: Ashgate, pp. 121–69.

Klein, L. (1984) 'The Third Earl of Shaftesbury and the Progress of Politeness', *Eighteenth-Century Studies* 18(2): 186–214.

—— (1986) 'Berkeley, Shaftesbury and the Meaning of Politeness', *Studies in Eighteenth-Century Culture* 16: 57–68.

Lakoff, R. (1973) 'The Logic of Politeness; or, Minding Your P's and Q's', in C. Corum, T. C. Smith-Stark and A. Weiser (eds) *Papers from the Ninth Regional Meeting*, Chicago: Chicago Linguistics Society, pp. 292–305.

—— (2003) 'The New Incivility: Threat or Promise?', in J. Aitchison and D. M. Lewis (eds) *New Media Language*, London: Routledge.

Langford, P. (1989) *A Polite and Commercial People: England, 1727–1783*, Oxford: Clarendon Press.

Larkin, P. (1988) *Collected Poems*, ed. A. Thwaite, London: Marvell Press; Faber and Faber.

Lawrence, D. H. (1960) *Lady Chatterley's Lover*, Harmondsworth: Penguin.

Leech, G. N. (1983) *Principles of Pragmatics*, London: Longman.

Mill, J. S. (1958) *Considerations on Representative Government*, ed. C. V. Shields, Indianapolis: Bobbs-Merrill.

Mugglestone, L. (2003) *'Talking Proper': The Rise of Accent as Social Symbol*, 2nd edn, Oxford: Oxford University Press.

Ofcom (2005) *Language and Sexual Imagery in Broadcasting: A Contextual Investigation*, research study conducted by The Fuse Group on behalf of Ofcom, September 2005, available online at <http://www.ofcom.org.uk/research/radio/reports/bcr/language.pdf> (accessed December 2006).

Paxman, J. (1998) *The English: A Portrait of a People*, London: Michael Joseph.

Rolph, C. H. (ed.) (1961) *The Trial of Lady Chatterley: Regina v. Penguin Books Limited: The Transcript of the Trial*, Harmondsworth: Penguin.

Sierz, A. (2001) *In-Yer-Face Theatre: British Drama Today*, London: Faber and Faber.

Truss, L. (2005) *Talk to the Hand: The Utter Bloody Rudeness of Everyday Life (Or Six Good Reasons to Stay Home and Bolt the Door)*, London: Profile.

Warner, M. (1996) *Monuments and Maidens: The Allegory of the Female Form*, London: Vintage.

Watts, R. J. (2003) *Politeness*, Cambridge: Cambridge University Press.

Williams, R. (1977) *Marxism and Literature*, Oxford: Oxford University Press.

Part I

The vulgar tongue

Chapter 2

'The indefinable something'

Representing rudeness in the English dictionary

Lynda Mugglestone

'I hope I have not daubed my fingers', the eighteenth-century lexicographer Samuel Johnson is said to have replied after being congratulated on the omission of rude words in his own *Dictionary of the English Language* (1755). Johnson's response, as well as the terms of this original commendation, already signal certain assumptions about the proprieties expected of the English dictionary. Johnson's use of *daub*, for example, clearly suggests the deleterious effects of contagion, as well as a sense of distaste. As he had stated in 1747 in his *Plan* for the dictionary, the 'chief intent' of such a work was 'to preserve the purity' as well as to 'ascertain the meaning of our English idiom' (1747: 4). Moreover, as Johnson added, it was the words and phrases found 'in the works of those whom we commonly style polite writers' which, in the dictionary, would provide 'proper' authority for usage. Even within the illustrative quotations which accompanied each entry, politeness was often affirmed as a dominant stylistic and cultural ideal. Under *ungraceful*, a citation from Addison commends 'the most exquisite taste of politeness'; Locke was used to praise 'politeness in language' in Johnson's entry for *carry*; Jonathan Swift combines politeness and linguistic propriety in the sentence which Johnson chose to include under *use* ('Nothing would be of greater use towards the improvement of knowledge and politeness, than some effectual method for correcting, enlarging, and ascertaining our language').

Politeness is, of course, double-edged, its qualities can be confirmed by its absence as well as its presence. Johnson was, for instance, neatly able to suggest other interpretations for the praise which his own omission of 'naughty words' received. 'What, my dears! Then you have been looking for them!' he retorted. As a careful reading of Johnson's dictionary moreover reveals, even 'polite writers' can touch on matters which are otherwise impolite. While *impolite* was itself excluded as an entry term, Johnson chose to include four lines of poetry from Sir John Suckling under *fart* ('Love is the *fart* / Of every heart; / It pains a man when 'tis kept close; / And others doth offend, when 'tis let loose'), while *piss* received apparent legitimization from Shakespeare himself ('I charge the *pissing* conduit run nothing but claret'). Johnson's accompanying definitions meanwhile maintained the decorum (and reticence) which politeness seemed to demand: 'to make water', he delicately noted of *piss*. *Fart* was defined by the similarly euphemistic 'wind from behind'.

These tensions within Johnson's *Dictionary* encapsulate some of the problems of lexicography when dealing with the complex issues of rudeness and taboo. To what extent should lexis of this kind find its way into general English dictionaries (rather than being marginalized, say, in specialist dictionaries such as Francis Grose's *Classical Dictionary of the Vulgar Tongue* (1785), or John Farmer and W. E. Henley's six-volume *Slang and its Analogues*, publication of which spanned the closing years of the nineteenth century and the beginnings of the twentieth)? Moreover, if such words are to be included, what level of explicitness should figure in the definitions with which they are provided? 'To give the definition; to explain a thing by its qualities and circumstances', Johnson's entry for *define* carefully stated. A citation from the philosopher John Locke, given as part of the supporting evidence for this word, nevertheless already indicates that definition is not always an easy or straightforward matter. 'Though defining be thought the proper way to make known the proper signification, yet there are some words that will not be defined', Locke warned.

The politics of polite definition – and the limits to which this could be taken – form a recurrent topos in English lexicographic practice. The use of Latin, in the decent reticence of a learned tongue, was one solution adopted by some of Johnson's contemporaries for elucidating the self-evident impoliteness of certain words. 'Vulgar' English was thereby able to be displaced by cultured erudition in the deliberately euphemistic deployment of another language altogether. '*Foeminam subagitare*', as Nathanial Bailey defined *fuck* in his *Universal Etymological Dictionary* (see further p. 31). 'Four-letter' words of this kind challenged definition not only in terms of their own elements of sociocultural taboo, but also because of the seeming impossibility of combining delicacy and decorum in their explication. Simple omission of the offending items, which obviated the need for definition at all, was another possibility (as in Johnson's decision when he came to consider these particular entries for his own dictionary).

Selectivity, in this and other ways, had, however, been an entirely deliberate principle of construction in the early dictionaries. The first monolingual English dictionary – Robert Cawdrey's *Table Alphabeticall* of 1604 – had contained *c*.3,000 entries; Bailey's *Universal Etymological Dictionary* contained *c*.44,000 words, Johnson's *c*.4,000 fewer. 'Choice was to be made out of boundless variety', as Johnson stressed of his own working methods (1755: A1ᵛ). For later dictionaries, such as the *Oxford English Dictionary* (*OED*), these issues were, however, to be more controversial as well as more problematic. In two lectures delivered to the London Philological Society in November 1857, Richard Chenevix Trench had, for example, outlined an entirely new definition of lexicographic practice, stressing both comprehensiveness and completeness as requisite ideals for the future *OED*. Rather than the 'principle of selection' which Johnson discussed in the Preface to his dictionary, the remit of this new dictionary was instead defined as that of the *'Lexicon totius Anglicitatis'* (Trench 1860: 64) – an objective 'inventory' of the entire contents of the English language in past as well as present. Precedents by which Johnson had subjectively refused to countenance words used by Hobbes ('because I did not like his principles') or by which particular forms were castigated merely on the basis of individual predilection (*shabby* was 'a word that has crept into conversation and low writing; but ought not to be admitted into the language', as Johnson noted with overt proscriptive intent) were here firmly cast aside. 'The lexicographer is a historian, not a critic', Trench decreed; 'The business which he has undertaken is to collect and arrange all the words, whether good or bad, whether they do or do not commend themselves to his judgment' (1860: 5). 'It is no task of the maker of [a dictionary] to select the *good* words of a language', as he averred in another maxim for modern lexicography (1860: 4).

As Trench's lectures made plain, it was inclusiveness – of 'bad' as well as 'good' – which underpinned the making of the *OED* (first published between 1884 and 1928 under the title *A New English Dictionary on Historical Principles*). The philologist Frederick Furnivall was particularly explicit on this score. Shepherding the dictionary through the 1860s and most of the 1870s, Furnivall forcibly rejected the notion that the dictionary should represent only the canonical discourse of the great and the good. 'Fling our door wide! All, all, not one, but all, must enter', he asserted; 'We have set ourselves to form a National Portrait Gallery, not only of the worthies, but of all the members, of the race of English words' (MP/Furnivall/1862: 3). The extraordinary comprehensiveness which resulted was apparent from the beginning. While the words between *A* and *Ant* had occupied 84 pages in Johnson's *Dictionary*, they constituted the whole of the *OED*'s first fascicle, published in 352 pages (each with three columns) in 1884. *Ant–Batten* would be issued in the following year (in a further 352 pages). The span of the alphabet would not be complete until 1928; the finished text of the first edition, as the *Times Literary Supplement* announced, consisted of 15,488 pages and 178 miles of type (as well as 500,000 definitions, and nearly two million quotations (Broadribb 1928: 277). On the other hand, even tallies such as these were not to mean that the rhetoric – and the reality – of inclusion would always be in perfect concord. While a range of words and senses were, for various reasons, omitted during the process of the dictionary's composition (see further Mugglestone 2005), politeness, together with its antonyms, would also lead to a number of compromises within the ideal of the inventory as set down at the very beginning of the dictionary project. 'Prudery's first line of defence', as Peter Fryer has perceptively stressed, lies in 'the regulation of speech' (1963: 19).

The inception of the *OED* in Victorian England was a case in point. 'Resembling or typified by the attitudes supposedly characteristic of the Victorian era; prudish, strict; old-fashioned, out-dated', as *Victorian* would later be defined in the 1986 *Supplement to the OED* edited by Robert Burchfield. Stereotypical Victorianism was not noted either for its openness or its inclusivity. While other contemporary discourses clearly existed (as the historian Lesley Hall confirms, a number of wide-ranging shifts in the public discussion of sexuality, contraception, and sexual taxonomy can be observed in the closing decades of the nineteenth century (see Hall 2000)), it was reticence – and restraint – which, conversely, were most often to characterize the popular image of the 'Victorian'. Nineteenth-century coinages such as *ineffables* and *indescribables* – both of which euphemistically referred to 'trousers' – concisely illustrate the problems of linguistic indirection which could result. 'Mr. Trotter . . . gave four distinct slaps on the pocket of his mulberry indescribables', as Dickens wrote in *The Pickwick Papers*, comically engaging with this discourse of semantic disguise. While *ineffable* as an adjective signified the sublime ('That cannot be expressed or described in language; too great for words; transcending expression; unspeakable, unutterable, inexpressible', as it was defined in the *OED*), as a noun this too could share in the practice of decorous concealment: 'Shoes off, ineffables tucked up' as the poet and schoolmaster William Cory had written in his journal in 1867, describing the experience of paddling in the River Taw (Cornish 1897: 196). *Unmentionables* too bore witness to this contemporary fondness for verbal substitution, being used by a range of writers throughout the nineteenth century to signify such linguistically delicate items as trousers and underwear.

The politeness of such terms was indisputable, and they certainly provided a useful resource in a variety of contexts when the inexpressible had, for whatever reason, to be expressed. Nevertheless, this was not to mean that the *OED* would fail to give a detailed definition for *trousers* when the relevant section of the dictionary was reached in the early years of the twentieth century. 'A loose-fitting garment of cloth worn by men, covering the loins and legs to the ankles; sometimes said to have been worn over close-fitting breeches or pantaloons; now applied generally to any two-legged outer garment worn by both sexes, and extending from the waist usu. to the ankles', as the entry explained. Specificity (and the demands of a work constructed on the basis of scientific and historical scholarship) means that, in this respect, the indescribable was indeed to be described for the purposes of reference and the wider aims of linguistic pedagogy. We might, however, also remark the discreet use of *loins* as part of this definition, a word which had already received a noticeably delicate form of elucidation when *Lock–Lyyn* had been published in October 1903. 'The part of the body that should be covered by clothing and about which the clothes are bound', as the relevant entry had stated with impeccable propriety.

As the nuanced ambiguity of this wording suggests (Which part of the body? Where precisely are the clothes bound?), even lexicographers who were publicly committed to the absolutes of descriptivism and the factual language of record could experience certain problems when required to mention that which was conventionally subject to silence. How much detail, for example, could one legitimately give in defining *loins* in Victorian England? The corresponding entry in, say, a twentieth-century dictionary such as the *Encarta World English*

Dictionary is far more to the point in its analysis of meaning: 'the hips and the front of the body below the waist, considered as the part of the body that should be covered and as the site of the sexual organs' (Rooney 1999). While the first edition of the *OED* therefore proclaimed its 'historical principles' on each and every title-page, it also rapidly becomes clear from such entries that the dictionary was itself, in certain respects, almost inevitably to constitute part of the historical coding of its own era. A quotation from *Punch* in November 1884 (the year in which the first part of the *OED* went to press) offers, for example, a useful note of caution on the parameters of nineteenth-century acceptability in these matters of language and polite representation. 'If it is absolutely necessary to call a spade a spade then it must be done in a whisper', as *Punch* declared in an article discussing the judicial need for 'delicate synonyms' in the course of an on-going prosecution at the Exeter Assizes ('Law in Lavender' 1884: 229). While the *OED* editors were therefore by no means *necessarily* to be afraid to call a spade a spade ('to call things by their real names, without any euphemism or mincing of matters; to use plain or blunt language' as the relevant entry affirms) there was nevertheless, as we shall see, a significant amount of whispering which can also be detected in a range of entries within this first edition of the dictionary.

This was, as might be expected, particularly the case with those words which, in various ways, impacted on the fraught areas of sex and anatomy, of swearing and profanity, or which were felt to infringe upon the cultural norms of the polite world. While such words were undoubtedly part of the 'inventory' which Trench had extolled, their proper definition frequently challenged accepted – and expected – proprieties. *Anus*, politely left out of Johnson's dictionary, was, for example, a word which early presented problems for the *OED*. While Bailey, as we have seen, appropriated Latin to convey the illusion of decorum in difficult definitions, James Murray – editor-in-chief of the *OED* between 1878 and 1915 – was often to appropriate another polite and learned discourse, that of science. In these terms, an *anus* was, he decided, best apprehended as 'The posterior opening of the alimentary canal in animals, through which the excrements are ejected'. The definition (and its dignified circumlocution) here neatly sidesteps any connection with human anatomy; animals have an anus while silence – at least formally – descends on the human equivalent.

The entry for *menstruation* – a subject of particular taboo in Victorian England (see Showalter and Showalter 1972) – makes still more determined use of science as linguistic safety net. This was 'the act or process of discharging the catamenia', as the definition confirmed, offering little illumination compared to the explicitness of modern lexicography ('monthly discharge from the womb: the monthly process of discharging blood and other matter from the womb that occurs between puberty and menopause in women and female primates who are not pregnant', as the corresponding entry in *Encarta* explains). Common modes of referring to menstruation (as the 'monthlies' or the 'curse') failed, however, to secure representation in the first edition of the dictionary at all. Still more delicate areas of human anatomy or sexual experience conversely received explications which only the most determined might penetrate. The *vulva* is the 'external organ of generation in female mammals', a *testicle* is an 'ellipsoid glandular bod[y]', while *copulation* is, according to the first edition of the *OED*, a term restricted mainly to Zoology (and applicable only in the act of reproduction). The semantics of words such as *alvine* (from Latin *alvinus*, signifying 'the belly') had to be combated in the entry for *excrement* which, as this indicates, neatly veiled the rudeness of reality within an all too dignified diction ('the alvine faeces or the waste matter discharged from the bowels'). *Orgasm* was, in particular, to present a triumph of non-specific indirection, being able, at least by implication, to apply to any area in the body. Given as a term confined to physiological usage, it is defined as 'Excitement or violent action in an organ or part, accompanied with turgescence; *spec.* the height of venereal excitement in coition'.

For the *OED*, such entries reveal the delicate lines along which definitions could at times be balanced. Science – and an attendant process of semantic obfuscation – could be used to provide the decorum (and legitimization) which impolite subjects might themselves lack, confining potentially distasteful topics to specific (and ostensibly highly restricted) spheres. Archaism was another useful technique when it came to the need to define other aspects of usage which challenged polite expression. The verb *to bog* was, for example, defined with commendable obliqueness as 'To exonerate the bowels'. The polysyllabic formality of the Latinate *exonerate* not only contrasts markedly with the colloquial verb it is used to define but also makes use of a sense which, as a later entry in the dictionary confirms, was itself virtually obsolete in general use: 'To discharge the contents of (the body, an organ), *esp.* by evacuation; *to exonerate nature, oneself*: to relieve the bowels. *Obs.*' A similar practice came into play for *scrotum* for which the *OED* definition made use of the term *tegument* – a form which, as Murray admitted in the relevant entry, was also 'Now *rare* or *Obs.*'.

It is euphemism – in origin a rhetorical figure which, as the *OED* records, 'consists in the substitution of a word or expression of comparatively favourable implication or less unpleasant associations, instead of the harsher or more offensive one that would more precisely designate what is intended' – that is, of course, at the heart of such practices in the first edition. While euphemism in this context inclines therefore to the adoption of learned registers which in themselves impede directness, its presence elsewhere in the dictionary can reveal the operation of a wide-ranging set of social and moral norms (as well as their attendant images of taboo). Certain entries can, for example, involve a conspicuous element of double-think as one struggles to decode the underlying meaning. *Adultery*, an entry which occurs in the very first fascicle of the dictionary, is, for instance, defined as 'violation of the marriage-bed'. Appropriate explication here depends on a transferred use of 'marriage-bed' to signify, as the fascicle *Mandragora–Matter* confirmed when it appeared 21 years later, 'marital intercourse, with its rights and duties'. While modern dictionaries are again strikingly to the point in this context ('extramarital sex: voluntary sexual relations between a married person and somebody other than his or her spouse', as *Encarta* states), the embedded semantics of the first edition of the *OED* instead incline to a didacticism – and moral prohibition – which is significantly removed from the neutrality formally espoused. *Violation*, for example, possessed a range of highly negative senses, encompassing defilement, rape, and desecration. The dictionary's definition of *prostitution* was similar. Factual objectivity was abandoned in favour of a definition which is explicit in its moral weighting: 'The offering of the body to indiscriminate lewdness'. The possibly even more impolite subject of lesbianism shares – or perhaps even extends – this discourse of transgression ('a woman who practises unnatural vice with other women', as the original entry for *tribade* in *OED1* explains).

Other long-standing taboos also gave rise to a conspicuous delicacy which – even if formally incompatible with the lexicographical agenda set out by Trench – was nevertheless entirely in line with that 'strong taste – or talent – for euphemism' identified by Fryer in his *Mrs. Grundy: Studies in English Prudery* (1963: 27). In spite of the sanitation reforms which also hallmarked the Victorian era, lavatories, for example, appeared to demand particularly circumspect treatment. A *lavatory* is, we are told, 'a privy', with no further elaboration being offered within its definition. While *toilet* was not in current use in the nineteenth century in this particular sense, the corresponding entry from the modern *Encarta* can again be used to offer something of the objective – and detailed – analysis which we might perhaps have expected: 'a fixture for disposing of bodily waste: a bowl-shaped fixture with a waste drain and a flushing device connected to a water supply, used for defecating and urinating'. The brevity of the *OED1* entry for *lavatory* is clearly at some remove, not only from the *Encarta* of the future but also from the 'fabric of fact' (Murray 1884: 509) – and the associated level of explicitness – at which the dictionary aimed.

Of course, it could be argued that no greater level of explicitness is demanded in this context since the word – and its contemporary meaning – were both well known. This was, for instance, the premise which underpinned the identical definition – as a 'beast' – given for creatures as disparate as *crocodile* and *cockatrice* in Cawdrey's *Table Alphabeticall* of 1604. Lexicographical practices of this kind had, however, been forcefully abandoned for the new dictionary of the Philological Society. Indeed, if we turn to other equally well-known forms – such indeed as *basin* – in the *OED*, we encounter definitions which engage in detail with the physical and semantic qualities of the item under discussion. The lengthy entry for *basin*, for example, opens with a precise anatomization of its appearance and role: 'A hollow circular vessel'; 1a 'A circular vessel of greater width than depth, with sloping or curving sides, used for holding water and other liquids, especially for washing purposes'.

Basins, however, were included within the realms of the polite while lavatories clearly weren't, a divide which prompts a conspicuous economy (and evasiveness) to come into play in defining the latter and its synonyms. If one was, for example, to fail to be satisfied with the two-word definition for *lavatory* in *OED1* and hence decide to look up *privy* (which, given the conditions of serial publication for the dictionary, would not appear for a further six years), one would find that this too attracted a range of euphemistic synonyms which again offer little elucidation of what one (impolitely) desired to know. A *privy* is, we are told, 'a necessary, a private place of ease', as well as 'a latrine'. If one turns to *necessary*, one is referred to *necessary-house*, a term which is defined once again as 'a privy' (as is *latrine*), thereby bringing the reader full circle and rendering one none the wiser. Other comparable terms such as *closet* offer little further assistance; the relevant sense is glossed as a *closet-of-ease* (a term which isn't in the first edition of the dictionary at all), as well as a *water-closet* (an entry which wouldn't be published until 1923). At this point, however, leaving Victorian reticence behind (and almost 40 years since the first part of *OED1* had been published), one can at last find a definition which reaches some form of comprehensiveness: 'A closet or small room fitted up to serve as a privy, and furnished with water-supply to flush the pan and discharge its contents into a waste-pipe below. Often abbreviated W.C. Sometimes applied to the pan and the connected apparatus for flushing and discharge; also, loosely, to any kind of privy'.

The real issues of linguistic politeness – and lexicographical editing-out – remained, however, in the domain of human sexuality, a subject which could often produce a head-on collision between the principles of the 'inventory' set forth by Trench, and potentially conflicting views about the decorums (and associated proprieties) which the dictionary should observe. The correspondence between James Murray and another lexicographer, John Farmer – the co-editor of another serially published dictionary, *Slang and its Analogues* (1890–1904) – is particularly illuminating in this context. Farmer's letters, for example, make all too clear that the neutrality of the lexicographer could, for a variety of reasons, swiftly founder on the perceived appropriacy (and lexicographical acceptability) of terms such as *condom* and *cunt*. Politeness, as he had found to his cost, was not just a notional construct in Victorian England. His compositors had walked out when required to set the entries for *cunt* and related words; the extant sheets of the relevant volume of *Slang* had subsequently been destroyed. While Farmer took the printers, Thomas Poultner and Sons, to court in June 1891 (and again in November of the same year, the jury having failed to reach a verdict on the earlier occasion), the case eventually went against him. Farmer was left with costs of £114 (a not insignificant sum at that date), as well as the desperate need to find another publisher so that his dictionary could reach completion (see Atkinson 2003: 3).

Farmer wrote in part to share with Murray his own lexicographical experiences, as well as to explore various solutions to what dictionaries – and dictionary-makers – should do in the recording of such impolite vocabulary.

Lexicographical decorum emerges as a prime concern. 'I have earnestly striven, where the Examples are Coarse, to deal with them decently', Farmer wrote in 1890 (MP/23/7/90), advocating a process of stylistic translation in the dictionary by which coarseness could be transformed into decency through the apt use of definition. Decency, as another letter explains, was often to reside in conspicuous indirection. 'I had already been casting about for devices for obscuring, as far as possible, any unpleasant words with which I have to deal', Farmer noted (MP/1/9/90), adding that he had decided to resort to giving the definition for particularly problematic words in Latin (a precedent already established, as we have seen, in Bailey's eighteenth-century work). This was a solution which the *OED* too would later adopt (at least in part), as in the entry for the manifestly impolite *twat*. Used by Robert Browning in the mistaken conviction that it signified some item of a nun's apparel ('Then, owls and bats/ Cowls and twats/Monks and nuns/in a cloister's moods/Adjourn to the oak-stump pantry!', as Browning had written in 'Pippa Passes' (1846)), the word demanded inclusion in the dictionary. Definition here – at least in English – apparently passed the bounds of all possible decency. Only a cross-reference to an embedded citation from Bailey's *Universal Etymological Dictionary* of 1727 (complete with its own Latinate obfuscation) is able to supply the necessary inferences for a determined reader of the *OED*: '1727 BAILEY vol. II, Twat, *pudendum muliebre*'. Latin was likewise explicitly commended in the truncated entry for *cock* when used to signify 'penis' ('The current name among the people, but, *pudoris causa*, not admissible in polite speech or literature; in scientific language the Latin is used'). Further contravening the *OED*'s principles on the provision of a historical record for each and every word, the entry for this sense of *cock* was, in the first edition, denied supporting citations at all.

In terms of definition, entries such as that for *twat* can appear paradoxical in an English dictionary. The deployment of a dead and classical language to define the vigorous colloquiality of one that, in certain respects, seemed all too alive can involve, as here, an all-too-conspicuous stylistic disjunction. Farmer's letters to Murray provide, however, a useful analysis of the deliberation which came to be involved in this form of linguistic subterfuge. While the aim in defining words such as *meritorious* or *confine* therefore remained that of encapsulating the precise set of sense-discriminations which relevant usage revealed, definition for these more impolite territories within the English lexicon was significantly different. As Farmer explained, the intention was, in fact, to incorporate 'language not "understood" of the people in definition of the coarsest words' (MP/23/7/90). It was a process which, by implication, traded on an assumed socio-cultural divide by which only the possessors of a privileged education might possess the linguistic facility to decode the underlying meanings – even if, by a further socio-cultural stereotype, it was the 'people' ('the mass of the community', as the *OED* notes) who were often seen as using such terms in the first place.

Lexicographical indirection in this respect serves, in effect, to reverse the principles which had informed the very first monolingual dictionary in English. In his *Table Alphabeticall* (1604) Robert Cawdrey had, in the interests of creating 'skilfull speakers' among his readership, glossed difficult (and often Latinate) loan-words with plain and native definitions. *Agitate* was hence defined as 'driven, stirred, tossed'; *expostulate* was glossed with commendable clarity as 'to reason, or chide with, to complaine'. In these sensitive linguistic territories, the *OED* can therefore be seen to adopt diametrically opposite strategies, filtering perceived challenges to propriety through a language in which the connotations of erudition (and respectability) were uncontested. Even this, however, could apparently prove too dangerous at times. Sense 5a of *coney*, for example, notes that the word could be used as 'a term of endearment for a woman'. For sense 5b (a synonym of *cunt*), the dictionary simply declares 'Also indecently', and leaves it at that.

Nevertheless, a decision to exclude rude or obscene lexis altogether was still more problematic. While this might have satisfied the kind of popular morality which would undoubtedly have been affronted by the provision of a full – and explicit – definition for words such as *coney*, by the same token, it also compromised the very identity of the *OED* as inventory. 'The whole subject is very difficult & forms my greatest anxiety', Farmer confessed on this matter with reference to his own dictionary (MP/1/9/90). Murray's anxieties were similar. Should a word such as *cunt* be included? There were certainly those in the Philological Society who thought so. The matter was hotly debated before it was finally decided to omit the word ('not without regret', as Murray wrote to a later correspondent on this matter (MP/4/9/99)). Silence similarly descended on *fuck*, in spite of its own historicity. The lexis of birth control presented another domain which – for the Victorian lexicographer – was beyond the pale of linguistic (and moral) propriety. Perceived obscenity in this context was, in fact, to elicit what is perhaps the *OED*'s most systematic policy of suppression (this is discussed in detail in Mugglestone, forthcoming). *Condom*, for example, 'was just too obscene', as James Dixon, one of the dictionary's most valued contributors, advised Murray (MP/6/12/88). Even if the historical record could be traced, the weight of moral opinion placed the word outside the decorums which the dictionary might legitimately (and politely) countenance.

These varied issues of politeness and their lexicographical representation can therefore be used to explore a number of tensions in the principles (and practice) which came to be applied in the making of the first edition of the *OED* – and not least in the ways in which the contrasting dialectics of historian and critic, so neatly separated by Trench in 1857, were once again brought into shared operation. A range of conscious omissions from the dictionary can hence be seen to occlude significant aspects of Victorian history and social change (especially in terms of birth-control, for instance), while the moral tenor of other entries served to impart particularly Victorian (and conservative) nuances to the nature of the dictionary as didactic text. In this respect, as in others, the ideal of the 'inventory' of English was inevitably subject to compromise in ways which rendered Trench's '*Lexicon totius Anglicitatus*' less than total in its final tally. The lexis of contraception remained prohibited within the dictionary until Burchfield's *Supplements* of the later twentieth century; the taxonomy of sexuality which, as Weeks notes, was another revolution within Victorian history (see Weeks 1989) was subject to a similar period of silence. Neutrality could remain remote in entries for words such as *prostitute*, *tribade*, or *masturbate* ('to practise self-abuse', as *OED1* affirmed in another entry infused with moral distaste). It is nevertheless by such means that the history of the *OED* can be seen to reveal its own historical truths, based in the wide-ranging effects of public mores and the complexities of contemporary taboos in the period of its first formation. Self-evident too is the very real difficulty of sustaining objective representation of a language in each and every facet of its use. 'Such is the fate of hapless lexicography', as Samuel Johnson had ruefully concluded in 1755; 'not only darkness, but light, impedes and distresses it; things may be not only too little, but too much known, to be happily illustrated'.

References

Unpublished sources

Murray Papers, Bodleian Library, Oxford.
MP/Furnivall/1862. F. J. Furnivall, *Circular to the Members of the Philological Society*, 9 November 1862.
MP/6/12/88. J. Dixon to J. A. H. Murray, 6 December 1888.
MP/23/7/90. J. S. Farmer to J. A. H. Murray, 23 July 1890.
MP/1/9/90. J. S. Farmer to J. A. H. Murray, 1 September 1890.
MP/4/9/99. Draft of a letter from J. A. H. Murray to J. Hamilton, 4 September 1899.

Published sources

Atkinson, D. (ed.) (2003) *The Correspondence of John Stephen Farmer and W. E. Henley on Their Slang Dictionary, 1890–1904*, Lewiston, NY; Lampeter, England: Edwin Mellen Press.
Bailey, N. (1721) *An Universal Etymological Dictionary*, London: J. J. and P. Knapton.
[Broadribb, C. W.] (1928) 'Our Dictionary', *TLS*, 19 April, pp. 277–8.
Burchfield, R. W. (1972–86) *A Supplement to the Oxford English Dictionary*, 4 vols, Oxford: Clarendon Press.
Cawdrey, R. (1604) *A Table Alphabeticall of Hard Usual English Words*, London: Edmund Weauer.
Cornish, F. W. (ed.) (1897) *Extracts from the Letters and Journals of William Cory*, Oxford: Clarendon Press.
Encarta (1999) *World English Dictionary*, ed. K. Rooney, Microsoft Corporation, London: Bloomsbury.

Fryer, P. (1963) *Mrs. Grundy: Studies in English Prudery*, London: Dobson.

Hall, L. A. (2000) *Sex, Gender and Social Change in Britain Since 1880*, Basingstoke: Macmillan.

Johnson, S. (1747) *The Plan of a Dictionary of the English Language*, London: J. and P. Knapton.

—— (1755) *A Dictionary of the English Language: In which the Words are Deduced from their Originals, and Illustrated in their different Significations by Examples from the Best Writers*, 2 vols, London: W. Strahan.

'Law in Lavender' (1884) *Punch* 2, 15 November, p. 229.

Mugglestone, L. C. (2005) *Lost for Words: The Hidden History of the Oxford English Dictionary*, London and New York: Yale University Press.

—— (forthcoming) ' "Decent Reticence": Coarseness, Contraception, and the *OED*'.

Murray, J. A. H. (1884) 'Thirteenth Annual Address of the President to the Philological Society', *Transactions of the Philological Society* (1882–84): 501–31.

Murray, J. A. H., Bradley, H., Craigie, W. A. and Onions, C. T. (eds) (1884–1928) *A New English Dictionary on Historical Principles*, Oxford: Clarendon Press.

Rooney, K. (ed.) (1999) *Encarta World English Dictionary*, Microsoft Corporation, London: Bloomsbury.

Showalter, E. and Showalter, E. (1972) 'Victorian Women and Menstruation', in M. Vicinus (ed.) *Suffer and Be Still: Women in the Victorian Age*, Bloomington: Indiana University Press, p. 38–44.

Trench, R. C. (1860) *On Some Deficiencies in Our English Dictionaries*, 2nd edn, London: John W. Parker and Son.

Weeks, J. (1989) *Sex, Politics and Society: The Regulation of Sexuality Since 1800*, 2nd edn, London: Longman.

Chapter 3

Poubellication

In the lexical dunny with the furphy king from down under

Valentine Cunningham

To consider slang is of course to descend into the lower depths of the language and culture. Where the 'low' speakers are audible. To go linguistically downwards, down under, and indeed Down Under, to where ordinary Australian English is spoken – the lingo celebrated by Eric Partridge, in his long 1953 essay 'Australian English', for its 'healthy, only very rarely lawless, contempt for the social strata of language'; its 'unconventionality: freedom, or the desire of freedom, from restraint'; its 'low-browism'; its 'marked', even 'excessive', 'dependence upon and use of slang in speech and even in writing'; its facility in and lack of self-consciousness about 'the coining and using of new metaphors or of "outlandish" speech' (Partridge 1960: 116, 117, 124, 125). Not Pomspeak then, the language that Barry McKenzie – Aussie hero of Barry Humphries and Nicholas Garland's legendary *Private Eye* strip-cartoon about this bloke from Down Under chundering his freespoken way around London's Earls Court – travelled thousands of miles to challenge by way of glorious linguistic foulness (so foul that even *Private Eye* eventually felt compelled to pull the plug on it; see Humphries and Garland 1988). An uninhibited foulness cheered on in linguistically self-conscious Aussie literature such as Kaz Cooke's joyously bad-mouthing novel *The Crocodile Club* (1997).

In *The Crocodile Club* one Selina Plankton has a friend called Miranda who is full of stories about people, including Chloe Futura, a hotel receptionist.

> Miranda had already told her [Selina] how Chloe's husband had died of apoplexy the previous year. He had accidentally read the Macquarie Dictionary definition of 'furburger' and died in hysterics, tears rolling down his cheeks, clutching a Big Whopper.
>
> (Cooke 1997: 77)

When quizzed about the episode Kaz Cooke was surprised to find *furburger* not actually in her copy of the 1988 second edition of Macquarie, the *Australian National Dictionary*, the one she assumes she must have consulted for her novel ('Perhaps they have just let furburger fade away, or popped it in the indecency cupboard'). But she did find it in the third edition (1998): 'noun colloquial, The female genitals during the act of cunnilingus; hair pie'.[1] The entry for **furburger** in the highly informative *Bloomsbury Dictionary of Contemporary Slang*, edited by Tony Thorne (1991), tells us that, like **fur-doughnut, furry hoop** and **fur pie** which it helpfully lists at the same place, *furburger* signifies the vagina. These are 'Expressions which have been part of the male repertoire of vulgarisms since the 1960s'. In the USA *furburger* and *fur pie* 'are sometimes used to refer to a female or females in general'. Under **hair-pie** – a noun for (a) cunnilingus and (b) the female genitals – *Bloomsbury* informs us that 'The phrase is a male vulgarism heard in Britain but more widespread in Australia and the USA'. The verbal vulgarisms of the USA always feature heavily in slang dictionaries, and studies of slang-formation always stress the USA as the greatest modern cooker of slang in English. But, evidently, Australia comes in a good second. Jonathon Green's huge *Cassell's Dictionary of Slang*, the biggest and best there now is, has '**furburger** *n.* [1960s+] the vagina, esp. during the act of cunnilingus since then it is "eaten" (cf. BACON SANDWICH n.; BEARD RIDE n.; BOX LUNCH n.). [FUR n. (1) + play on SE *hamburger*; note synon. RMC Duntroon (Aus.) *muffburger*]'. Since the late sixteenth century, Green tells us, **fur** has been used for female pubic hair, and since the eighteenth century for the vagina. **Muff** has meant vagina and pubic hair since the seventeenth century, and as a verb in the twentieth century came to mean to perform cunnilingus. Green's entry for **muff-dive** (also **muff-nosh**), a verb originating in the USA in the 1940s meaning to perform cunnilingus, asks us to 'note RMC Duntroon (Aus.) *muffdive*, the act of cunnilingus'. RMC Duntroon is the Australian Royal Military College at Duntroon, whose language is reported by Bruce Moore (editor of the *Australian National Dictionary*) in *A Lexicon of Cadet Language: Royal Military College, Duntroon, in the Period 1983 to 1985*.[2]

Kaz Cooke's arrestingly Rabelaisian, Bahktinian moment, in which a piece of coarse linguisticity is cheerfully savoured, and where writing happily engages with language unperturbedly engaging with the lower parts of the body and with physical activities widely deemed unrespectable and doing so in the coarsest of terms, namely a vile term taken from that very large family of disturbing slangy metaphors for male sexual activity and sexual use of women involving rough, violent, exploitative, crude eating or consuming by mouth – in other words, this bit of low mouthing about low-down mouthwork – is, of course, Australian. An Australian novel makes comically free with a word for what's somatically down under taken from the low slang lexicon which gets so many cheerful mouth-outings Down Under.

Which is publication – *Australian* publication – as *poubellication*. *Poubellication*: Jacques Lacan's neologism for utterances and publications that go wrong, are rubbishy in some way, or are deemed so, and get rubbished, ending up in the *poubelle*. *Poubelle*: the French word for dustbin or trashcan, named, in a piece of affectionate slang, in memory of Monsieur Eugène Poubelle, prefect of the Seine district of Paris, 1883–96, who organised the Parisian rubbish collection, and gave his name to what my old French–English dictionary of 1923 (rescued by me with what now seems some aptness from my school rubbish-heap) describes as the 'dust-box placed before every house in Paris to be emptied daily'. The *poubelle*: it's where, as it were, slang users assemble and slang collects: in those mean parts of town where slang is spoken and generated, in fictions about them such as *The Crocodile Club*, and, most blatantly of all, in dictionaries of slang. For the slang dictionary is a kind of *poubelle*: where the linguistic trash is gathered, the filthy words, the linguistic waste-matters of the culture, the vocabulary of the gutter and of gutter people, those citizens deemed to be social trash, the marginals and outsiders and the outcast, crooks and villains and transgressors, men transported to Botany Bay, homosexuals, gipsies, the soldiery, seamen, pedlars, Billingsgate fishwives, East-Enders, flash coves, loose women and bad boys, all those word-users suspected of being people with ill-intent and things to hide, malevolents full of moral malaises, speakers whose vocables and tones are despised as uneducated and illiterate, whose mouths need 'washing out' because they're filled with words considered as too noisome for polite and respectable discourse and respectable company and respectable occasions. The words thought of as variously rude and crude, coarse, filthy, bad, vulgar, smutty, lewd, blasphemous, heretic, improper, obscene.

So the garnerer and collector of this noxious stuff, the maker of the slang dictionary, is a *poubelliste*, but a *poubelliste extraordinaire*, because he – this lexicographer is mainly a he – is the linguistic dustbin-man who wants not to ditch and discard his containers of linguistic *Abfall*, to bury and burn his carefully garnered low materials away from the haunts of clean and civilized folk, to quench this verbal crap's dismaying pongs and annihilate its allegedly harmful potencies, but who wants by contrast to save and conserve it, to keep it in view. His wish is to publish and publicize this dire material, in fact, as document and record and an exhibition of just how prevalent and pervasive it has been and is.

At the core of *poubelle* lexicography, of lexicography as *poubellication*, are, naturally enough, the allegedly very low words, the phrases and metaphors, for the lower parts of the body and the activities associated with those somatic nether regions, the impolite lexicon for pissing and shitting and fucking, for what the euphemistically inclined refer to as what goes on 'down there', all the unrespectable lingo for the life of 'down there' deemed to be so socially and culturally and ethically low that it struggles perennially to enter not just the world of respectable language use but also the pages of the respectable mainstream dictionary. All of which is the special preoccupation of the master *poubelliste*, the lexicographical maestro of this low material, the Down There King himself, namely Eric Partridge, the greatest modern garnerer of slang, the language-recording fanatic who worked almost single-handedly to bring home to the English just how pervasive filthy English has been and still is, to reveal how much English and English speakers have been and are preoccupied with the lower parts of the body and with 'low' actions and behaviour expressed in a 'low' fashion. Eric Partridge: the lexicographer who is, inevitably I'd say, from Down Under.

He was born 6 February 1894 on a farm in the North Island of New Zealand; migrated with his family to Brisbane, Queensland, Australia, in 1907; got much childhood reading pleasure from his father's dictionaries; attended Toowoomba Grammar School until he was 16, taught for four years in schools in Queensland and New South Wales, won a Classics scholarship to Queensland University. At the end of his first year in April 1915 he enlisted in the Australian Army, trained with the Australian Imperial Force in Egypt, served in the Anzac horror of Gallipoli, came to France with the Second Australian Division, was wounded in the great Somme offences of 1916 in the Division's 'Second Pozières' attack of 4 August. He was hospitalized in England, then returned to France where he served, despite patent nervous damage and emotional frailty, right to the end of the conflict. After the war he returned to studies in Australia, switching from Classics to French and English. In 1921 the Queensland Government Foundation Travelling Scholarship brought him to St Catherine's College, Oxford, for a BLitt on 'The Influence of English Literature Upon the French Romantics'. He got the degree in January 1924; the thesis was published that year as *The French Romantics' Knowledge of English Literature (1820–48)*, along with *Eighteenth-Century English Romantic Poetry, up till the Publication of the 'Lyrical Ballads'* – his Queensland MA thesis which he had managed to complete in Oxford in 1923. Unassiduous he was not.

After a few weeks back home in 1924 Partridge returned to England for good. He did bits of tutoring in Oxford; taught at Hulme Grammar School in Manchester (for seven months); was a junior lecturer in English at Victoria College, the future University of Manchester (1925–6); lectured in English at London University (1927–8). But he was never happy lecturing, and he was soon making his way rather as a Man of Letters, a maker of books, the freelance writer living entirely by his pen. He tried his hand as a novelist, became a successful literary journalist, became a publisher (and self-publisher), founding the Scholartis Press at 30 Museum Street, in Bloomsbury, opposite the British Museum, in September 1927. Beavering away in the British Museum Reading Room (soon notorious as the scruffy bookworm always at Seat K1), he turned himself into England's most renowned writer on language and compiler of lexicons (a way of life modelled a lot, he would admit, on the example of Ernest Weekley, the Nottingham language professor whose books like *The Romance of Words* (1912), *The Romance of Names* (1914) and *An Etymological Dictionary of Modern English* (1921) greatly popularized the subject of English words). And for Partridge it was not just any old language or lexicons, but the language that caused so much trouble for Ernest Weekley's former pupil D. H. Lawrence (he who ran off with Weekley's wife Frieda), namely slang. The low stuff: the language of the lowly, language at the level of the lowest of the low, language epitomized in *Lady Chatterley's Lover*'s insistence on using the so-called four-letter words *fuck* and *cunt*. Words from below, from below the salt, below stairs, from out of the trench and the dug-out and the closet, from down under and Down Under. The language precisely of Partridge's own kind and of his war-time acquaintance, language from where he had been for three terrible years, with the men from Down Under, the soldiery of and from the colonial margin (that iconic and extreme case of provincial separation and otherness), the descendants of the cockneys, the whores and criminals, of Magwitch and his mates, banished with their low behaviour and low mouths, to Sydney Cove and Botany Bay, who returned to Europe in the Great War in such great numbers bringing their linguistic freedoms and verbal uncouthnesses – and their recorder Eric Partridge – with them. The loud return of the linguistically repressed.[3]

Partridge relished, he said, the uninhibited linguistic life of the lower Australian rankers (he refused a commission several times):

> As a private, I learned much more about Australian speech, about Australian English, than I could possibly have done as an officer. I was meeting all the roughs and the toughs, as well as many decent fellows coming from trades and professions of which I knew nothing – or so little as to be worse than nothing. Although I had earned my living since I was sixteen, I had, as teacher and then as undergraduate, met only a few different types of mankind: now I was meeting all conceivable types, from the wealthy pastoralist to the petty crook; from the cane-cutter to the 'wharfie'; from the rural storekeeper to the urban shopkeeper; from the book-keeper to the bookmaker; from the journalist to the 'sundowner' and the 'swaggie'; from the Civil Servant to the commercial traveller and the 'con man' proper; from the shearer to the sailor; from the railway official to the tram-driver. Not only meeting but living with them, in conditions where men regard modesty and reticence as unwanted luggage. Having a quick ear, a comparative mind, a retentive memory, and no hesitation in asking for full and precise information whenever I was in doubt and could ask without giving offence, I naturally acquired a considerable store of technical and semi-technical standard Australian English, as well as a not inconsiderable stock of slangy and colloquial and other unconventional words and phrases and senses and idioms.
>
> (Partridge 1963: 13–25; reprinted in Partridge 1980: 41–50)

He'd happened upon one of the great social cookers of slang (when the Second World War broke out he knew precisely where to head, notebook in hand – volunteering for service in the Army Education Corps (1940–1) and the Correspondence Department of the Royal Air Force (1942–5)). In this accidentally-arrived-at happy hunting ground for the slang-*poubelliste*-to-be began his lifelong addiction with underworld discourse and rhetoric of all sorts: the obsessive missionary crusade to record the words of every possible class of ne'er-do-well, outcast, marginal and provincial – the language of Manchester and of Nottingham's D. H. Lawrence, it might be, the kind of words gathered in the lexicon Partridge was dotty about, namely poor-boy Bradford lexicographer Joseph Wright's *English Dialect Dictionary* (1898–1905) – the speech exemplified particularly in the uncouth talk of colonials and soldiers, especially the colonial soldiery. Partridge would speak for the socially silenced by loudly and repeatedly voicing their peculiar and special words and phrases, uttering out loud what the respectable deemed unspeakable, bringing edged-out words into the lexical centre, resurrecting the verbally repressed, bringing socially and ethically dark sayings out into the light – the light, at least, of the word-book, the lexicon, the public word-hoard of the slang dictionary.

Partridge's language mission was, arrestingly, a strong and particular version of the extraordinary story of twentieth-century English philology, which was utterly commanded by scholarship boys from Down Under, all those New Zealanders and Australians who spoke for the history of the English language in Oxford – the likes of Kenneth Sisam, J. A. W. Bennett, Eric Dobson, Norman Davis, Bruce Mitchell, Douglas Gray: a covey of Partridge types who, as it were, turned Partridge in the person of one of their number, the New Zealander (and veteran of the Second World War) Robert Burchfield, who as editor of the great four-volume *Supplement* to the *Oxford English Dictionary* finally admitted *bugger, come, cunnilingus, fellatio, French letter, frig* and *fuck* and similar uncouthisms to what is now the *OED*'s second edition. (Nor is it accidental that this radical lowering of the *Oxford Dictionary*'s tone was done under the auspices of Dan Davin the then publisher of the Oxford University Press, yet another New Zealander and old soldier, the official historian of the Second New Zealand Expeditionary Force's action in Crete, who invited fellow-New Zealander Burchfield to edit the new Supplement.[4])

The earliest public signs of Partridge's interests in soldier-speak are in 'A Mere Private', a long autobiographical story about his military career in the Australian ranks, not least on the Somme and in the Pozières attack in which he was wounded, published with other autobiographical narratives in *Glimpses*, under the pseudonym Corrie Denison by his own Scholartis Press in 1928. It's laced with the code of the trenches, the dialect of the British Tommy and his Australian comrades – carefully quoted along with embryonic socio-philological notations. The 'disgraceful' affair of the Somme assault of July 1916 'was the origin of the cynical remark that one so often heard applied to absentees at informal roll-calls of the unlucky battalions involved (a saying that soon spread to other units): "Hanging on the barbed-wire" ' (Denison 1928: 119). False rumours were rife; Harry, the Partridge character, 'collected all the "pferfies" (as they were known to the Australians) he could' (108). He rejoiced when he heard that his thigh wound 'was "a Blighty one" as the Tommies used to say, "a Blighty" in the terser slang of his countrymen' (127). Harry's great friend Phillips, assigned the fruitier vocabularies of the rougher-mouthed Australians,

> used language so startling, so biting, so realistic that whenever he began
> cursing, all within ear-shot ceased from talking in order to listen to this

wonderful, horrible flow of words, as rapidly varied as it was uniformly picturesque, with English, American, Spanish and Australian terms intermingled . . . a volcanic luridness and power . . . foul, scorching, sardonically humorous outbursts.

(Denison 1928: 90)

On the slang front, *Glimpses* was followed by *Songs and Slang of the British Soldier, 1914–1918*, a co-operative volume composed with John Brophy (Eric Partridge Ltd at the Scholartis Press, 1930). Brophy – a Liverpudlian war-novelist and advertising-copywriter who had enlisted at the age of 14 and served in France – took care of the Introduction and the songs, Brophy and Partridge the glossary, with Partridge supplying the Australianisms. The glossary, filled out with social and historical detail and personal reminiscence, notably on the Anzac front, was pretty mild in its choices (*Pferfies*: army rumours; *Anzac*: a synonym for the Australian and New Zealand troops and derived from Anzac Cove, Gallipoli; *Digger*: Australian term from the gold-fields; *diggers* meant Australian troops and, among the Brits, New Zealanders). But there were also signs of sharper things to come with *Hot Stuff, Jig-a-Jig, Knocking Shop, Latrine Rumour, Piece, Pump Ship* ('urinate': sailor's slang), as well as an entry on *Rhyming Slang* and the direction the entry for *Scrounge* pointed in (old pre-war word, North Country dialect, as reported by Joseph Wright's *Dialect Dictionary*).

By 1931 Partridge was cutting looser in Godfrey Irwin's *American Tramp and Underworld Slang: Words and Phrases Used by Hoboes, Tramps, Migratory Workers and Those on the Fringes of Society, with Their Uses and Origins* (Eric Partridge Ltd at the Scholartis Press, once more). His 'A Terminal Essay on American Slang in its Relation to English Thieves' Slang' historicizes keenly, slathering the would-be prude with evidence of long-life slanginess. *Tail*, meaning buttocks and sexual intercourse in modern American, 'occurs in English literature from the 14th century onwards, for the *membrum* and, much more often, the *pudendum*, and occasionally for a harlot' (Irwin and Partridge 1931: 264). *Hump, screw* and *shag* get particular attention. For evidence of the vintage of these words for copulation Partridge calls on Francis Grose's *A Classical Dictionary of the Vulgar Tongue* (1785), but he's also especially keen to give them Great War provenance: '*Screw* and *shag* were both used by British soldiers, in 1914–18, to mean sexual intercourse and its corresponding transitive verb' (263). These old soldier's provenances would be a constant.

By now you could see the lay of Partridge's lexicographical land: interests and strategies vividly confirmed in the same year by *A CLASSICAL DICTIONARY OF THE VULGAR TONGUE BY CAPTAIN FRANCIS GROSE EDITED WITH A BIOGRAPHICAL AND CRITICAL SKETCH AND AN EXTENSIVE COMMENTARY BY ERIC PARTRIDGE, M.A., B. LITT. (OXON.)*, 'Issued for Private Subscribers by the Scholartis Press'. (It's dedicated to Professor Ernest Weekley, 'AS BRILLIANT AS HE IS ENTERTAINING'.) The 'commentary' is Partridge's extended annotations of Grose. Characteristic is the little essay on 'TO F – K. To copulate': 'Banned by OD and EDD [Oxford and Joseph Wright]. Used by Lyndsay *ca*. 1540, and occurring in Florio's definition of *fottere*: "To jape; to sarde, to fucke; to swive; to occupy".'(*A Worlde of Wordes, or, Most Copious, and Exact Dictionarie in English and Italian* (1st edn, 1598) by Elizabethan Italian Protestant John Florio, the great guide to Elizabethan and Shakespearian colloquialisms, would be much cited by Partridge in these uncouth connexions.)

> One of the last occasions on which it ['F – K'] appeared in print, in the ordinary way of publication, was in Burns. . . . It is extremely doubtful if the efforts of James Joyce in *Ulysses* and D. H. Lawrence in *Lady Chatterley's Lover* have done anything to restore the term to its former place as a language-word, i.e. neither slang nor dialect. . . . From Greek *phuteuo*, L. *futuere*, Fr. *foutre*, the medial *c* coming from a Teutonic root. Sir Richard Burton, in his Arabian Nights, attempted a Gallic twist: *futter*. – The synonyms (on the basis of F [J. S. Farmer & W. E. Henley's *Slang and its Analogues* (1890–1904): a much used source]) are numerous in accredited literature exclusive of slang, euphemism, and conventionalism. . . . The vivid expressiveness and the vigorous ingenuity of these synonyms bear witness to the fertility of English and to the enthusiastic English participation in the universal fascination of the creative act. The word was very much used by the British Soldier in 1914–1918 (see the Introduction in B & P [*Songs and Slang of the British Soldier, 1914–1918*]), when free currency was also given to the adjective formed by the addition of *ing* and to *f – ker;* this latter, in the mouths of the fouler-spoken, meant little more than chap, fellow, and the decent substituted *mucker; mucking* was less frequent.
>
> (155–6)

Partridge's way was now established. Ancient indelicacies – here 'PRICK', 'BLOOD', 'C**T', 'ARSE', and the like – would be given scholarly back-stories, roots, provenances, all updated with reference to the modern soldiery's usages. Here was a linguistic treasure trove from the British Museum library afforced by the Anzac's trooper's field-work in the field.

> Until *ca.* 1700, it [ARSE] was quite respectable English. Frederic Manning was considered extremely audacious (January 1930) to use the word in his supreme war-novel *Her Privates We*. – The word ('obsolete in polite use' says the OD in 1888) had long served in dialect for the bottom or hinder part of anything as in *sack-arse*. EDD. – As a C19 slang verb it meant transitively: to kick; intransitively: to depart, move away. In 1914–1918 soldiers used the verb transitively to mean: to kick out, to dismiss, e.g. 'He was arsed out of his job,' and intransitively as in 'to arse about,' to fool

about, to waste time; some people think this phrase is merely *ass about*, to play the donkey, the fool, as in many instances – but not in the soldiers' – it certainly is.

(19–20)

The edition of Grose was followed in 1932 by *Literary Sessions* (Eric Partridge Ltd at the Scholartis Press once more). It reprints symptomatic Partridge pieces like the one on 'Scurvy' (165–9) turning in by now quite predictable directions ('We often speak of malpractice as a *shabby* or *scurvy trick*' (165); had Richard Brookes, the great eighteenth-century authority on scurvy 'lived in 1914–1918 he would have seen people, here and there, getting scurvy through the inadequacy of the supply of butter and fat' (168)). After this came *Words, Words, Words!* (Methuen, 1933: Scholartis having evidently ceased trading), with Partridge really hitting his stride in a fetching set of subversively truth-telling essays. There's 'Euphemism and Euphemisms' ('The parts of the body . . . have suffered gravely from this false modesty' (99); the 1914–18 war-time has generated an agreeable loosening of speech: since then 'it has been yearly becoming more permissible to speak of *brothel, prostitute, procurer, pimp* and *syphilis*' (101)). And 'Rhyming Slang, Back Slang, and Other Oddities', about those kinds of low, Cockney lingo which have travelled well Down Under ('Back slang has always been peculiar to Cockneys, although they have not tried to confine it to London; back slang reached the Colonies – well, fifty years ago at least' (36)). And 'The Word Bloody' (the real selling-point of the volume, some of Partridge's friends told him), greatly expanding the 'Blood' entry in the Grose, with especially more detail about the Great War soldiery ('*Bloody* was their favourite adverb and adjective: all other "swear words", frequently as some were used, might be described as "also-rans". It even served as an intersyllabic or intervocalic word, as in "im-bloody-possible" or "too bloody right" ' (86)). 'Soldiers' Slang of Three Nations' is a lovely comparative collection of English, French and German words and phrases from the trenches. For instance:

> *Latrinen-befehl, -gerucht*, and *-parole*, latrine-order, -rumour, -password – and, late in the War, just (*eine*) *Latrine* – the English term being latrine-rumour, the latrine member being sometimes expressed in vulgarism. The French generally use the word *tuyau*, a pipe, but they also have *mamelouk*, a circularizer of rumours; *perco*, from percolateur . . . Other English terms are *gup*; *Furphy*, an Australianism.
>
> (200–1)

In an extended Appendix II, 'Some Groups of "Tommy" Words', Partridge gathers groups of 'army slang words of 1914–18 . . . that are particularly reminiscent of the trials and humours of the times; certain terms, certain phrases, smelling still of earth and fear, filth and eager experience' (211), words from the men 'Down in their *dug-outs*' (213), not least vulgarisms pertaining to lower bodily functions, words with the smell, as it were, of bodily filth on them.

> One kind of *eyewash*, the army's innumerable 'states' and 'returns', was known as *bumf*, short for *bum-fodder*: the abbreviation was common in English public schools from before 1900; the full term for toilet-paper dates back to the seventeenth century, when it was coined by Urquhart, the translator of Rabelais; Urquhart is one of the most prolific originators of the obscenities and vulgarisms of our language, and with him rank Shakespeare and Burns. The proper 'stage' for the use of bumf was the *jakes*, etymology doubtful; but perhaps the word, as the O.E.D. suggests, represents *Jack's house, place*, and it has been in use for at least four hundred years. The official name was *latrine*, from Latin *latrina*, a lavatory. The rumours that flew about so gaily were often called *latrine rumours*, more vulgarly *s--- -house rumours*; less offensively they were known as *transport tales, cook-house yarns, shaves* (old Regular Army), or, among the Australians, *furphies*, from *Furphy*, a relevant contractor at Melbourne. The naval equivalents are *cook-house official, cook's-galley yarn, forecastle wireless* (post-war), and *galley-packet*. The activity of the cooks is obvious. *Jakes* reminds us of two curious terms of assent: *jake* and *jake-a-loo*. Colonial troops employed them thus: 'It's jake *or* jake-a-loo', it's correct, genuine, true, no hoax.
>
> (211–12)

Coming the old linguistic soldier (specialty Colonial) was clearly coming most naturally to Partridge. 1933 also saw his *Slang To-Day and Yesterday: With a Short Historical Sketch and Vocabularies of English, American, and Australian Slang* (George Routledge & Sons). It was commissioned by another old soldier Colonel F. C. C. Egerson, then Routledge's chief editor. Its essays on 'Colonial Slang' include large accounts of South African, Canadian and New Zealand slang, as well as Australian. New Zealand slang ('the most conservative of all the colonial slangs': it used, say, *kidney pie* for 'insincere praise' where the Americans used *bull* and Australians *bullsh*, 'and both, in less hurried moments, *bull-sh-t*') tended, Partridge observes with a note of regret, to get submerged into Australian: 'During the War (as before and after it), whenever a New Zealand slang term became famous or very widely used it was discovered to be equally or more famous or widely used among the Australians' (Partridge 1933a: 285–6).

By 1933 Partridge was hard at work on what was to become his most momentous lexicographical achievement, the great *Dictionary of Slang and Unconventional English: Slang – Including the Language of the Underworld, Colloquialisms and Catch-Phrases, Solecisms and Catachreses, Nicknames, Vulgarisms and Such Americanisms as Have Been Naturalized*, the first edition of which was published by Routledge in 1937. An enlarged second edition followed in 1938, a 'much enlarged' third edition in 1949, a fourth 'revised' edition in 1951, and then in 1961 came the fifth edition, in two volumes, 'much enlarged', incorporating all the Addenda of the second to fourth editions into Volume I and adding a *Supplement* of 'mainly . . . new words and phrases', the most important part of which 'is the slang of World War II'. By then *A Dictionary of Slang* had become a life's work, the greatest machine for recording the history and presence of uncouth English there had ever been, a treasure-house of low usage. Here was the linguistically uncouth in rich heaps, especially words and phrases – new ones, old ones, dialectical survivors, bright new spins on the old tropes – dealing exuberantly, as slang does, with lower body parts and functions: *bump*, *bugger*, *buttered bun* (woman having sex with several men in quick succession), *catso* (penis), *come*, *cunt*, *silly cunt*, *cunt-itch*, *cunt-hat* (a thing that's *felt*: double pun, as Partridge points out), *dilberries* ('Impure deposits about the anus or the pudend'), *dildo* ('exchange sexual caresses with a woman'), *dirty work at the crossroads*, *fuck*, *hump*, *hole*, *jiggling bone*, *jet one's juice*, *jerk off*, *jesuit* (sodomite), *a bit of meat*, *pistol* (penis), *poke*, *poke hole*, *pole*, *prick*, *you silly prick*, *quim*, *quim-bush*, *quim-whiskers*, *quim-wedge*, *quim-sticking*, *rush up the straight*, *saddle*, *stand* ('erectio penis' and 'mouth-whore'), *do a squeeze*, *do a squirt*, *squirt one's juice*, *short and thick like a Welshman's prick*, *shoot up the straight*, *shooter's hill* (cunt), *shit-hunter* (sodomite), *screw*, *suck* (noun, homosexual), *suck-and-swallow* (cunt), *tail*, *ladies' tailoring*, *she goes as if she cracked nuts with her tail*, *she lies backwards and lets out her fore-rooms*, *tip the velvet*, and so on and on. A rude assembly, richly peopled by antipodean usage (Australian mainly, but shading over into New Zealand), as for instance: *blue* and *bluey* (drunk), *bugger about*, *dunny* (a privy, Australian since *c.* 1880), *go crook*, *full as a tick*, *grafter*, *hard stuff*, *hump* (carry, shoulder, as *hump one's swag*), *full as an egg*, *goo-goo eyes*, *kangaroos* (West Australian mining shares; dealers in these), *have for breakfast*, *lag* (convict; Dickens's Artful Dodger is *lagged*, i.e. transported for life), *lag-ship* (convict ship), *lagging and a lifer* (transportation for life), *lamb-down* (to make a man get rid of his money to one; to spend while in drink), *hatter* (miner working on his own), all the *mag* (swindler, confidence trickster) words, *possum-guts*, *sheila*, *shicer* (unproductive claim; a defaulter), *shicker* (get drunk), *dinkum* (noun, work; adjective, true, genuine), *fair dinkum* (fair play, carried over from Lincolnshire dialect), *the dinkum oil* (the truth), *post-and-rail tea*, *shivaroo* (spree, party), *slant* (plan or scene of operations designed to effect a favourable result), *slanter* (unfair), *snag* (formidable opponent), *stiff* (certain to win, penniless, unlucky), *toe-ragger*, *tucker* (eatables, originally gold-diggers' rations), *wowser* (puritan, spoil-sport), *yellow-fever* (craving for gold), *yoxter* (a convict returning to England before his time: a Magwitch), *stagger-juice*, *down* (prejudice against, hostility toward). Colloquialisms these, all rooted so to say in a huge abundance of militarisms from the Great War: *Ballocky Bill the Sailor* ('most generously testicled'), *hanging on the old barbed wire*, *great life if you don't weaken*, *have a good look round for you won't see anything but the ceiling for a day or two* (words of soldiers on leave re. spouses: 'cf. *feet upper-most*'), *have by the short hairs*, *do* (military offensive), *do a bishop* (parade at short notice), *do one's bit*, *FA* (from *Fuck All*, as in *sweet Fanny Adams* or *sweet FA*), *you are slower than the second coming of Christ*, *hardware* (ammunition, shells), *hate* (bombardment), *footslogger*, *sandbag* (cosh made from sausage-shaped bag of sand: 'It leaves almost no mark; often employed by soldier deserters or gangsters on Salisbury Plain and on the Etaples dunes during the G[reat] W[ar]'), *jigger* (front-line trench), *shit* (mud; bombardment, especially with shrapnel), *in the shit* (in mud and slush, in great and constant danger), *show*, *whizz-bang*, *strafe*, *stunt*, *shag* ('Very gen[eral] among soldiers in G[reat] W[ar]'). An army of militarisms in which the particular slang of the Anzac soldier is prominent: *Anzac* itself, *Arse-ups* (the 4th Battalion of the New Zealand Rifle Brigade), *bint* (Arabic for girl, picked up in Egypt), *gor-blimey* (old cockneyism, adopted for a service cap), *boozer*, *china* (mate, from cockney-rhyming *china plate*), *dingbats*, *digger*, *up the digger*, *Jewel of Asia* (Dardanelles gun), *Jericho Jane & Asiatic Annie* (Turkish guns), *kangaroo* or *Anzac poker* (confidence-tricksters' card-game: 'Prob[ably] introduced by Australian soldiers in 1915, when hundreds of them were evacuated, wounded, from Gallipoli to England'), *pozzy* (Pozières), *parapet Joe* (German machine-gunner playing tunes along the parapet, '*pom-tiddley-om-pom pom-pom* being the usual burst'), *shrapnel* (NZ for low denomination French currency), *sand-bag duff* (NZ: pudding made from ground biscuit), *spud-barber* (NZ: man on cook-house fatigue), *my colonial oath*, *stoush* (Aussie for fighting given particular military spin: 'anything from fisticuffs to a great battle'), *Zionist* (the Zion Mule Corps at Gallipoli). An army of Anzacisms in which louche vocabulary from and for lower-bodily ways and means is peculiarly prominent: *soldiers! I've shit 'em* (contemptuous phrase for another unit), *soldier's joy* (masturbation), *finger*, *finger-fuck*, *fun* (fundament), *fur*, *furbelow*, *furze-bush*, *furphy*, *furphy king*, *goo-wallahs*, *hole*, *better ole*, *latrine rumour*, *frig*, *frigging*, *frig-ster*, *frigstress*, *frills*, *frisk*, *piss-quick*, *pisser*, *pistol* (penis), *bugger* (noun), *bug-ger* (verb), *bumf*, *cunts in velvet* (the CID), *fuck*, *fucker*, *fucking*, *Fuck you Jack I'm all right*, *a soldier's farewell* (= 'Goodbye and bugger – or fuck – you'), *a good look round* (sex on leave). And so on and so forth.

The steady expansions of the *Dictionary* indicated, of course, the way Partridge's greed to acquire and explain and bring to the right-minded and respectable reader's ear and eye the verbally uncouth never let up. He couldn't resist featuring and promoting these low interests. They surface everywhere. In, for instance, his handily pocket-sized anthology of 1938, *For These Few Minutes: Almost an Anthology* (Arthur Barker, 12 Orange Street, London, WC2), that reproduces his essay on some French Great War terms, 'A Poilu Trio' (which, of course, features the slangy *système dé*, meaning something like a 'wangle', short for *système débrouille*, or *démerde*, the wily ways of the *démerdeur* or soldier full of the handiest kind of shit, 'picturesquely' put (Partridge 1938: 408)). Partridge's 1940 booklet *Slang*, SPE [Society for Pure

English] Tract 55, one of the clearest guides ever to slang origins and categories, comes expectably rich with cases from the military and the RAF of 1914–18 and after, including, naturally, Australian ones (*bonza, cobber, dinkum, go West* (Partridge 1940: 191)). Australian usage is, as ever, on his mind: the tract's few Cockney illustrations include '*barrikin*, chatter, especially if unintelligible; shouting; whence the Australian cricket-slang, *barracking*, now accepted by Standard English' (188). His little *Dictionary of RAF Slang* (Michael Joseph, 1945), and the *Dictionary of Forces' Slang, 1939–1945*, by Wilfred Granville, Frank Roberts and Partridge (Secker & Warburg, 1948) – Partridge did the Air Force section – nicely indicate Partridge's nose for where the good slang hangs out. (The *Supplement* to the *Dictionary of Slang* is markedly full of Canadian and Canadian military slang contributed by Canadian informers eager not to appear outdone by the Americans and Australians.) His '1949' volume *A Dictionary of the Underworld: British & American: Being the Vocabularies of Crooks, Criminals, Racketeers, Beggars and Tramps, Convicts, the Commercial Underworld, the Drug Traffic, the White Slave Traffic, Spivs* (London: Routledge & Kegan Paul Ltd, 1950) enthusiastically revisits the old stamping grounds of Grose, and *American Tramp and Underworld Slang*, as well as *A Dictionary of Slang*, in keenly updating mode.

Partridge was, of course, never one to miss a possible book-making trick, but his constant repetitions and returns and recastings of the same or similar linguistic materials – which include the wonderful wartime essays reprinted in *Words at War: Words at Peace: Essays on Language in General and Particular Words* (1948): 'War as a Word-Maker: Some Foreign Words War-Introduced or War-Popularized in 1880–1938'; 'Army Slang with a Shady Past'; 'Words Get Their Wings: The Slang of the Royal Air Force'; 'Cant: The Language of the Underworld' – are more than just a reflection of the freelancer's need to keep churning out the articles and books. They indicate his abiding sense of the nature of slang and its origins in the world of the low, the underworld, especially epitomized for him in the military with whom he spent the Great War, in particular the mouth-work of the Anzac fighting-man, the descendants of the Cockney exiles deported down under, the sons as it were of Abel Magwitch, the transported convict in Dickens's *Great Expectations* (1860–1).

The antipodean convict territory, where the dialect of Dickens's proletarian, criminal Londoners flourished, because that's where it had been transferred to, is deep down, in every sense. Magwitch's contact man in London, the lawyer Jaggers, is 'Deep as Australia', according to his clerk Wemmick – 'Pointing with his pen at the office floor . . . ' (*Great Expectations*, ch. 24). 'Tell us your name! . . . Give it mouth!', the terrifyingly uncouth Cockney Magwitch commands little Pip at the beginning of Dickens's novel. Deported, Magwitch and his kind *gave it mouth* Down Under. His kind was Bill Sikes's kind. 'Only . . . an initiate like Bill Sykes' [*sic*] – this is Partridge on 'Cant: The Language of the Underworld' – 'would know the meanings of the cant words for acquiring, taking, seizing, stealing; for running away, breaking prison, escaping; for burgling, swindling, arson, kidnapping, shooting, killing; for arresting, sentencing, imprisoning, hanging . . . ; for informer, policeman, detective, lawyer, judge', and so on and on: the low vocabulary flourishing everywhere, but not least, as Partridge indicates in this piece, in Australia.[5]

Why Magwitch? The *Dictionary of Slang* records a whole clutch of nineteenth-century *mag* words, all criminally inclined: *mag*, to steal; *on the mag*, on the lookout for victims; *mag-stake*, money got by confidence trickery; *magsman*, street swindler or confidence trickster. It's clear where *magsman* Magwitch got his name: from the crookedly derived word for men you can't trust who went to Australia and stayed on.

This is the vocabulary for badness and of bad people – so-called. Filthy talk of, by and about filthy people and filthy things – so-deemed. The slang lexicon is a *poubelle* unembarrassedly laden with the 'filthy' language of the kind of human being exported Down Under because they were deemed morally and socially filthy. (A *filth* was a harlot from Shakespeare on, according to Partridge's *Dictionary of Slang*.) R. W. Burchfield reports the revulsion of some Oxford lexicographers wanting nothing to do with 'Partridge and his filth' when it came to putting the banished words into the *OED*. Dickens was of similar mind about Australian slang. (He was actively involved in rescuing London prostitutes and sending them to Australia for a new life, like Martha Endell in *David Copperfield*. Many of his fallen women refused to go, making 'a fatal and decisive confusion between emigration and transportation' (letter of 12 April 1850, Dickens 1988: 83).) In his great *Household Words* article 'Slang' (24 September 1853), Dickens acknowledged – and greatly deplored – the colonial sources of slang. These degenerate linguistic imports are bidding fair to 'debase, and corrupt that currency of speech which it has been the aim of the greatest scholars and publicists, from the days of Elizabeth downwards, to elevate, to improve, and to refine'. If, he continued, 'we continue the reckless and indiscriminate importation and incorporation into our language of every cant term of speech from the columns of American newspapers, every Canvas Town epithet from the vocabularies of gold-diggers . . . the noble English tongue will become, fifty years hence, a mere dialect of colonial idioms, enervated ultramontanisms and literate slang'. What was coming in was linguistic filth:

> The fertility of a language may degenerate into the feculence of weeds and tares: should we not rather, instead of raking and heaping together worthless novelties of expression, endeavour to weed, to expurgate, to epurate; to render, once more, wholesome and pellucid that which was once a 'well of English undefiled,' and rescue it from the sewerage of verbiage and slang? The Thames is to be purified; why not the language?
>
> (73)

Sewage; *weeds and tares*; *feculence*, i.e. shitty, faecal matter, *raked* up into *heaps*. And Dickens produces pages of examples of the noisome verbal stuff 'we' are 'dabbling' in, naming the various sources of the slang that is 'dirtying the stream' of the English language: New York, New Orleans the 'crescent city', 'Brigands, burglars, beggars, impostors, and swindlers' (74), mariners, actors, literary critics, men in clubs, men on racecourses, navvies. His long list of examples he produces, he says, with no effort at all. The reading public will be able to supplement it easily: the 'evil' 'jabber' of slang, this 'vulgar' 'gibberish', this 'low language', is so prevalent. And the list is growing all the time, growing with the growth of the colonies, expanding with the docking of every colonial mail-boat. And Australia is so large a source it gets special mention. 'The arrival of every mail, the extension of every colony, the working of every Australian mine would swell it [the list]. Placers, squatters, diggers, clearings, nuggets, cradles, claims – where were all these words a dozen years ago?' (76). And now in the early twentieth century that feculence was arriving in a quantity Dickens could not have imagined, with the great Great War's invasion of the Anzac common soldiery – whose very uncommon mate, and ardent recorder, was Eric Partridge.[6]

Feculent words, then, from the social, geographical, moral, and lexico-graphical *periphery* (Partridge's own word for these places of linguistic banishment) – or what had been forcibly constructed as the periphery, the Magwitch edge of the respectable world. The vocabulary specialized in by the unrespectable Aussie and Anzac where words like *fur* for female pubic hair (generic head of the linguistic household into which *furburger* would be born) lived on after their banishment from polite English circles. To return, or be returned by, the Aussie soldiers from that periphery and their recorder. *Fur* (low), says that Anzac trooper's *Dictionary of Slang*, 'The (gen. female) pubic hair', eighteenth–twentieth century, just one of the huge number of as it were saved and rescued words from the socially and geographically far below and describing the bodily far below. Like the neighbour of *fur* in Partridge: *furbelow* (seventeenth–nineteenth century), 'female pubic hair'. *Furbelow* – nicely echoic of *far-below* – word from the socially far below, for the female hair from the bodily below, no longer, now Partridge is having his way with it, concealed and banished to the lexical far below. This is precisely the vocabulary the Digger from the Anzac dug-out will diligently dig out. And then put into his lexical *poubelle* – or, as he and his Anzac kind would say, his lexical *Furphy cart*.

Furphy: it was the Anzacs' very own word for a kind of military *poubelle* and *poubellication*, an exemplary colloquialism from the Anzac trenches and thus in Partridge's revelations. It derived from the iron carts made by Methodist local preacher John Furphy's foundry at Shepparton, Victoria, with the name Furphy painted prominently on their sides, made familiar to the Australian soldiery at the Broadmeadows army training camp at Melbourne. These *Furphy carts* seem to have been versatile containers, transporting water but also, it appears, sewage and possibly other sorts of rubbish. Amanda Laugesen maintains in her edition of *Diggerspeak* that the carts were only for water (Laugesen 2005: 91); Jonathon Green's second edition calls them 'sanitary carts'; the second edition of the

OED has 'water and sanitary carts'. Partridge focuses on the rubbish and shit collection function. His *Dictionary* claims Mr Furphy was 'the contractor supplying rubbish-carts to the camps at Melbourne'. *The Anzac Book: Written and Illustrated in Gallipoli by the Men of Anzac* (1916) agrees: 'Furphy was the name of the contractor which was written large upon the rubbish carts that he supplied to the Melbourne camps'.[7] (That sounds like Partridge's source: the fact that he spells them 'pferfies' in his early fiction indicates he never saw one, only heard the word from his Australian comrades.) The Australian word-list in *Slang: To-Day and Yesterday* calls Furphy a 'sewage-contractor'. In the Aussie ranks a *furphy* was a baseless rumour, a word for all the false stories busily circulating through the army, a characteristic of military life (and one of the most abiding gifts of the Anzacs to modern Australian English). A *furphy* is a kind of verbal rubbish, in fact; it's talking *ballocks* (= *nonsense*, according to Partridge's *Dictionary*; soldier talk for *muddle* after 1915, as the *Supplement* informs), or *talking shit* (as the 1910s+ phrase has it, according to Jonathon Green's second edition). What Partridge calls, in the passage from 'Some Groups of "Tommy" Words' quoted above, *latrine-rumours* or *shit-house rumours*. For him the eponymous Mr Furphy is the 'relevant contractor at Melbourne' because it's his shit-collection carts that have given their name to the slangy military's customary word for verbal rubbish. *Furphies* – at least on Partridge's reading – are *shit-house rumours* by association with the latrines where gossip flourished and rumours circulated, and the Furphy carts stood waiting to collect the excrements. Hence Partridge's *Dictionary*: *latrine rumour*: 'False news: a wild story; a baseless prediction: military: 1915. Ex the fact that latrines were recognised gossiping places'. Furphy, latrine-rumour, shit-house talk: the very stuff of the slang dictionary – the lexicographical Furphy Cart.[8]

Here's Partridge filling up the Furphy Cart of Grose in the entry for 'SH–T SACK', 'A dastardly fellow':

> *Shit* and *shite* are both noun and verb, though the latter form is not, except in dialect, often used of the noun. The verb dates from *ca.* 1300; the noun from *ca.* 1500, since when, indeed, it has been a term of contempt for a man. OD. – In 1914–1918 the soldiers used either *shit* or *shit-house* of any unpopular person (very rarely of a woman); they used it also as an expletive, cf. Fr *merde!* But both these uses had been pre-War. Pre-War was *in the shit*, in trouble; but a specifically military application was: in the mud and slush, in mud and danger, in great or constant danger; and *shit* meant also shelling, especially shelling with shrapnel. – Dialect has many expressive senses and phrases, as e.g. *shitten*, *shitten-like*, *shit-arsed fellow*, paltry, contemptible; *to be always either of height or of shite*, to be extremely variable of temper and spirits. EDD. – The OD itself admits *shit-house*, *shit-fire*, (a hot-tempered person: pejorative), and the obsolete *shit-word* (abuse), all now ranking as vulgarisms.
>
> (307–8)

Once more the soldier who had been *in the shit* and wounded by *shit* at Pozières speaks out in the voice of the freespoken Second Australians, men full of the vocabulary which is the Slang Furphy Cart's usual contents. Vocabulary, the slang historian easily demonstrates, as old as the hills, and everywhere in the literary tradition, the canon, before the Bowdlerizers tried to pretend otherwise. Anzac-speak, Magwitch's lingo, the shit-house talk of Gallipoli and the Somme is Shakespeare's own. Which is the point of Partridge's *Shakespeare's Bawdy* (1947) – that great overturning, critically revolutionary work of serious challenge to the Bowdlerizers of the Bard, to every Bardolatrist deluded enough to think England's most canonized playwright clean in thought and language, to every pedagogue wanting to shut his pupils' ears to the filthy talk of the Master: the Slang lexicon as potent lit crit. In which it's not difficult to detect a lot of sympathy for Shakespeare's stroppy old soldier, the Ancient Pistol, in *2 Henry IV* (named, as the *Dictionary of Slang* enjoys learnedly pointing out, for 'the male member', as in Florio's *pistolfo*).

'A foutre for the world and worldlings base!', Pistol exclaims at *2 Henry IV*, V.iii.98, and 'A foutre for thine office!' at V.iii.114. Pistol doesn't give a fuck for the officer class nor for polite ways of expressing that resistance, as any ranker would not, especially an Anzac. Partridge warms to the point.

> **foutre,** n. As an imprecation: '*Pistol.* A foutre for . . . A foutre for . . .'
>
> Fr. *foutre*, 'to coït with (a woman)'. Pistol's 'a foutre for' has its exact equivalent in modern English vulgarism: *a fu*k for!*
>
> *Foutre* is from L. *futuere* (perhaps cognate with Gr. *phuteuein*).

Like all slang dictionaries *Shakespeare's Bawdy* doesn't give a fuck for polite lexicography. As the slang lexicon reclaims the dictionary for historical and empirical truth about language, so *Shakespeare's Bawdy* reclaims the literary glossary. Partridge's counter-lessons from linguistic history now get focused as counter-literary critical ones. Much like in the (and I would say not accidentally) Australian Latinist J. N. Adams's wonderfully illuminating lexicon of the filthy words peopling Latin literature, *The Latin Sexual Vocabulary* (1982) – where, of course, the commonest low Latin word for male sexual congress, *futuo*, I fuck, gets its deserved star billing. A *foutre* all round for polite literary history.

It should not be thought that thus defying the codes and conventions of *politesse* came easily. Diggerspeak, the 'Dinkum Australian' of the First World War, observed one old Aussie soldier, rightly, 'has three very marked properties – Forceful, Expressive, and Unprintable' (quoted in Laugesen 2005: x). Getting the unprintable into print – defying the kind of resistance reflected in the *Oxford Dictionary*'s long kept-up refusals, and in the prosecutions of *Ulysses* and D. H. Lawrence's novels – was a slow process. Partridge's own long struggle to perfect his Somme material indicates something of the strain of getting the soldierly words up from underground.[9] *Songs and Slang of the British Soldier,*

1914–1918 omitted several songs 'as unprintable' – according to the advertisement in *American Tramp and Underworld Slang*. The contents of *Songs and Slang* come prefaced by John Brophy's extended diatribe against the 'three very ugly words around which almost all Army obscenity revolved'. War slackened 'the inhibitions of speech' too much. 'Most men who served in the Army were coarsened in thought and speech. . . . The agents of this corruption of the mind were these three obscene words, uttered in every other sentence when soldiers spoke amongst themselves'. Brophy can't bring himself to utter *bugger*, *cunt* and *fuck*, but they are evidently the blackguards in question. *Lady Chatterley's Lover*'s vile twosome – the unsayable *fuck* and *cunt* – 'rear their unlovely heads out of the page, gibbering abominably'. The ugliness of these old words satisfied men in the ugliness of war – the recent war which exaggerated the large ugliness of 'modern urban civilization'. These words

> come from the stews of cities; vents for the exasperation of the slum-born and slum-bred . . . they are the refuge of the *un*natural man, of the unfortunates overstrained by poverty or war, and of the poor creatures who cannot make a job of marriage but must stimulate their jaded desire with secret harlotries and mindless shows of dancing girls. The man to whom circumstance allows some cleanliness, peace and order, and who centres his life on his wife and children, has no need of these curse words and despises them.
>
> (Brophy and Partridge 1930: 15–19)

This is Brophy, not Partridge, but it does indicate the hot contemporary resistance to Partridge's desired outspokenness. The fact that the Grose edition was published for Private Subscribers only, and even then went in for dashes and asterisks, and that *fuck* and *cunt* attracted asterisks in the early editions of the *Dictionary of Slang* are, I take it, rather symptoms of fear of the law than of Partridge's personal mealymouthedness (even though the *Dictionary*'s original preface was never dropped, with its talk of 'unpleasant terms' needing 'aseptic' treatment, and how in a few instances 'I had to force myself to overcome an instinctive repugnance' (Partridge 1937b: x)). Partridge's lifetime of slang evangelizing and missionary work speaks for itself. But the way of the slang lexicographer in the first two thirds of the twentieth century was evidently hard. And Partridge, to his great credit, persisted in it. And right to the end.

The last thing that I know he published is a *Times Literary Supplement* review of G. A. Wilkes's *Dictionary of Australian Colloquialisms* (18 August 1978) that showed him gamey about low usage to the end (he died 1 June 1979). He defends his use of 'low' and 'vulgar' in the *Dictionary of Slang* ('The lowest common denominator remains the lowest' (Partridge 1978: 933)). He's still the testifying New Zealander obsessed with low Australianisms ('No, I'm not Australian-born; merely one of those New Zealanders so oddly prominent in the lexicography of Australian speech' (934)). An obsessive still glorying in the

Aussie soldiery's catchily low inventiveness: those 'jocular replies' to enquiries about someone's whereabouts – *hanging on the old barbed wire* from the Great War, of course; *gone for a crap on the padre's bike*, from the Second. This is latrine, or *dunny* talk: as fun, and as fundamental, for Partridge as it ever was. The first example from Wilkes he brings up for delighted scrutiny is *All alone like a country dunny*. It is for Partridge a quintessential Aussie catchphrase, yet one more as it were insanitary one, vividly encapsulating, as he has long wanted us to believe such catchphrases do, a world of vital Australian experience. Here's the loneliness of the outback resident dweller Partridge and his people once were, and the primitive sanitary arrangements of his old Aussie country-side. Wilkes dates the phrase to 1952. But *dunny*, says Partridge, is no new-comer; it's the vocabulary of the original convict settlers, and as low-down and earthy as the human race they talked for. *Dunny*, from *dunnaken*, then from *dannaken* (as the *Dictionary of Slang* had long explained), the place of dung, especially human dung. A gypsy word, brought westwards from Hindi and Sanskrit, getting into London underworld speech, it travelled to Australia 'with the First Fleet in 1788'. It survived and thrived in Australia, and now, as ever, Partridge – lexical *poubelliste* and *furphy-king* or *dunny-man* to the last, still hauling along his lexical *poubelle* and *furphy-cart* or *dunny-cart* (Aussie version of *danna-drag* or *dunnaken-drag*, 'the night man's cart' as the *Dictionary of Slang* has it) – Partridge insists on its being heard, in all its rich Australianized identity, the word from and for the outside dung-house which uninhibited Australianism still keeps happily alive.[10]

Notes

1 I owe my knowledge of *The Crocodile Club* to Australian lawyer Michael Hall who regaled me one lunchtime with this tragi-comic moment of death by rudely hilarious lexicographical acquaintance when I happened to mention to him the story 'The Furburger', which is a funny North American tale about a wife's revenge on her husband by means of a creature called a 'furburger' – in Angela Carter's collection of rude stories about triumphantly rude and free-speaking females, *The Virago Book of Fairy Tales* (1990: 92–3). He very kindly asked his friend Kaz Cooke for me about that fatal definition.

2 I'm grateful to Jonathon Green for his information about Moore's Duntroon *Lexicon* and for many other pointings in useful directions regarding Aussie slang.

3 Details of Partridge's life come from Partridge 1963: chs 1, 2; Partridge 1937a: 312–17; Geoffrey Serle's 'Introduction' to Partridge 1987; Green 2004.

4 Burchfield (1989: 189) pinpoints the New Zealand connexion in 'The *OED*: Past and Present'. His article, 'Four-Letter Words and the *OED*' (1972), about these impolite introductions, intriguingly quotes the 1969 correspondence between the editors of *OZ* magazine, complaining of the omission of *fuck* from the *Shorter Oxford English Dictionary*, and Dan Davin, who assures them of the future inclusion of 'this and similar words' in the new *Supplement*. *OZ* was a satirical 1960s magazine started in Australia by Richard Neville and exported to London. Neville was found guilty at the Old Bailey of 'corrupting public morals' with a *Schoolkids OZ*, and sentenced to 15 months in jail and deportation to Australia – conviction quashed on appeal. It's

notable that Burchfield was goaded by Raymond Williams's allegations in his *Keywords: A Vocabulary of Culture and Society* (1976) of ideological bias in the *OED* to assert his personal lexicographical credentials as *inter alia* a working-class scholarship-boy old-soldier from New Zealand (Burchfield 1976).

5 'Cant: The Language of the Underworld', *The Nineteenth Century and After* (January 1943); reprinted in Partridge 1948: 171–6.

6 In his essay on Australian Slang in *Slang To-Day and Yesterday* Partridge is at pains to stress that Dickens has failed to observe that *claim* is equally American and Australian and that *clearing, placer* and *squatter* were American before they were Australian, but he can't quarrel with their actual Australianism (Partridge 1933a: 290).

7 Explanatory footnote to story, 'Furphy', by Q.E.D. (*The Anzac Book*, 1916: 56).

8 I am indebted to Barry Collett, Australian historian, for filling me in on the continuing life of *furphy* Down Under.

9 The 'Frank Honeywood' story began as on-the-spot notes kept in the trenches and in letters posted home, was drafted up in hospital in England (September–October 1916), published in the *Queensland University Magazine* (October 1918), expanded in *Glimpses* in 1928, revised again in June–July 1929, published in *Three Personal Records* (October 1929), and polished even further for inclusion in *A Covey of Partridge* (1937): details in Partridge 1987: 9.

10 Partridge 1978: 933–4. *Hanging on the old barbed wire* is in Partridge's last book, *A Dictionary of Catch Phrases: British and American from the Sixteenth Century to the Present Day* (1977), and singled out for special mention as a 'serious' catch phrase in the Introduction. *Gone for a crap on the padre's bike* is not, but the RAF equivalent, *gone for a shit with a rug round him*, is.

References

Adams, J. N. (1982) *The Latin Sexual Vocabulary*, London: Duckworth.

The Anzac Book: Written and Illustrated in Gallipoli by the Men of Anzac (1916) London: Cassell.

Brophy, J. and Partridge, E. (1930) *Songs and Slang of the British Soldier, 1914–1918*, London: Scholartis Press.

Burchfield, R. W. (1972) 'Four-Letter Words and the *OED*', *TLS*, 13 October, p. 1233.

—— (1976) 'A Case of Mistaken Identity', *Encounter*, June, pp. 57–64.

—— (1989) *Unlocking the English Language*, London: Faber and Faber.

Carter, A. (ed.) (1990) *The Virago Book of Fairy Tales*, London: Virago Press.

Cooke, K. (1997) *The Crocodile Club*, St Leonards, NSW: Allen & Unwin.

Denison, C. [i.e. Partridge, E.] (1928) *Glimpses*, 2nd edn, London: Scholartis Press.

Dickens, C. (1853) 'Slang', *Household Words* 8(183), 24 September, pp. 74–8.

—— (1988) *The Letters of Charles Dickens*, Pilgrim edn, vol. 6: 1850–2, ed. G. Storey, K. Tillotson and N. Burgis, Oxford: Clarendon Press.

Green, J. (2004) 'Partridge, Eric Honeywood (1894–1979)', *Oxford Dictionary of National Biography*, Oxford University Press, available online at <http://www.oxforddnb.com/view/article/31531> (accessed November 2006).

—— (2005) *Cassell's Dictionary of Slang*, 2nd edn, London: Weidenfeld & Nicolson.

Grose, F. and Partridge, E. (1931) *A Classical Dictionary of the Vulgar Tongue*, ed. E. Partridge, 2nd edn, London: Scholartis Press.

Humphries, B. and Garland, N. (1988) *The Complete Barry McKenzie*, London: Methuen.

Irwin, G. and Partridge, E. (1931) *American Tramp and Underworld Slang: Words and Phrases Used by Hoboes, Tramps, Migratory Workers and Those on the Fringes of Society, with Their Uses and Origins*, London: Scholartis Press.

Laugesen, A. (2005) *Diggerspeak: The Language of Australians at War*, South Melbourne, Victoria: Oxford University Press.

Macquarie, (ed.) (1988) *Australian National Dictionary*.

Moore, B. (ed.) (1993) *A Lexicon of Cadet Language: Royal Military College, Duntroon, in the Period 1983 to 1985*, Canberra: Australian National Dictionary.

Partridge, E. (1932) *Literary Sessions*, London: Scholartis Press.

—— (1933a) *Slang To-Day and Yesterday: With a Short Historical Sketch and Vocabularies of English, American, and Australian Slang*, London: Routledge.

—— (1933b) *Words, Words, Words!*, London: Methuen.

—— (1937a) *A Covey of Partridge: An Anthology*, London: Routledge.

—— (1937b) *A Dictionary of Slang and Unconventional English: Slang – Including the Language of the Underworld, Colloquialisms and Catch-Phrases, Solecisms and Catachreses, Nicknames, Vulgarisms and Such Americanisms as Have Been Naturalized*, 1st edn, London: Routledge.

—— (1938) *For These Few Minutes: Almost an Anthology*, London: Barker.

—— (1940) *Slang*, SPE Tract 55, Oxford: Clarendon Press.

—— (1945) *Dictionary of RAF Slang*, London: Joseph.

—— (1947) *Shakespeare's Bawdy: A Literary & Psychological Essay, and a Comprehensive Glossary*, London: Routledge.

—— (1948) *Words at War: Words at Peace: Essays on Language in General and Particular Words*, London: Muller.

—— (1950) *A Dictionary of the Underworld: British & American: Being the Vocabularies of Crooks, Criminals, Racketeers, Beggars and Tramps, Convicts, the Commercial Underworld, the Drug Traffic, the White Slave Traffic, Spivs*, London: Routledge & Kegan Paul.

—— (1960) *A Charm of Words: Essays and Papers on Language*, London: Hamish Hamilton.

—— (1963) *The Gentle Art of Lexicography as Pursued and Experienced by an Addict*, London: Deutsch.

—— (1977) *A Dictionary of Catch Phrases: British and American, from the Sixteenth Century to the Present Day*, London: Routledge & Kegan Paul.

—— (1978) 'As Australian as a Meat Pie', *TLS*, 18 August, pp. 933–4.

—— (1980) *Eric Partridge in His Own Words*, ed. D. Crystal, London: Deutsch.

—— (1987) *Frank Honeywood, Private: A Personal Record of the 1914–1918 War*, ed. G. Serle, Carlton, Victoria: Melbourne University Press.

Partridge, E., Granville, W. and Roberts, F. (eds) (1948) *Dictionary of Forces' Slang, 1939–1945*, London: Secker & Warburg.

Thorne, T. (1991) *Bloomsbury Dictionary of Contemporary Slang*, London: Bloomsbury.

Williams, R. (1976) *Keywords: A Vocabulary of Culture and Society*, London: Fontana.

Chapter 4

Rude words

Tom Paulin

More than 50 years ago, my parents moved from Leeds to Belfast. They bought a house in a terraced street, North Parade, off the Ormean Road, in south Belfast. My parents tell me I had a Yorkshire accent then, and I can remember that the language the other children in the street spoke was at first strange to me. I was four years old in a city with a strange name, which comes from the Irish *beale*, *mouth* and *Farcet*, the river Farcet, one of the rivers the city is built on.

It had to be explained to me that 'three D' – pronounced 'thhee dee' – meant thruppence (these were the days of LSD, pounds, shillings and pence). Sweets were 'jubjubes', an ice-cream wafer was a 'slider'. The word orange – as in 'orange squash' – was pronounced 'ornj'. Many years later, I read a letter of Hopkins in which he describes his fascination with the northern Irish pronunciation of *r*:

> Making *apple* and *arrow* in Chaucerian style one syllable has a quaint charm, the charm of learned archaism; still I think it wrong, and inconsistent with the rest of the scansion. In no modern pronunciation of English could *apple*, I think, be monosyllabic (except of course if a vowel followed and the *e* were swallowed – like *appl' and pear*). *Arrow* on the other hand might here in Ireland become a dipthong, the *r* before a vowel being not trilled or rolled as in England but burred or 'furred' and half lost, so that the sound is like *ah-o* and almost *ow* (they say 'the marge and buryal of an Ornge barster in Meryon Square', that is, *the marriage and burial* etc.); and nearly this, no doubt, was Chaucer's sound, but you cannot well take your ground on that.
>
> (Hopkins 1955: 156)

Hopkins uses the Elizabethan pronunciation of 'hour' – 'hower', as it appears in *Dr Faustus* – in the sonnet that begins 'I wake and feel the fell of dark, not day': He then says:

> What hours, O what black hoürs we have spent.
>
> (Hopkins 1967: 101)

The second time he uses 'hours' he adds an umlaut to signify that it is two syllables, and this thickens and lengthens the word and the time it designates. Hopkins makes the word resonant and desperate. We need to recognize that there are vernacular and local pronunciations at times in Hopkins – 'God rest him all road ever he offended!' in 'Felix Randal' is meant to be voiced in a Lancashire accent.

When I think back to those early days in Belfast, I realize that I came into a rich, spoken vernacular which used words that might broadly be defined as 'rude'. By a rude word, I don't mean a word that has some kind of sexual reference, or that is bad-mannered, but a word that is not part of a polished, standard English, and which often carries a witty sense of its unpolished, quirky, less-than-couth qualities. But as Hopkins's letter implies, much English poetry has its roots in this oral, dialectical language.

All children speak self-consciously, partly to show that they're in the know and are also daring and confident. In the city I came to, sectarianism shaped parts of the language – I discovered that there were catholics and protestants – teagues and prods – and that I was a protestant. Though we went to separate schools, we played together on the street and on the 'half', the cross street that ran from South Parade across North Parade to Park Road. It ran from a school called Ulidia – a state and therefore protestant school – whose name was strange to us, though I recall a friend telling me it was Irish for 'Ulster'. It ran from Ulidia to the Ormeau Park.

When I consider my early experience of Ulster English, I realize that I had the good luck to grow up inside an energetic oral language which used words we never saw in print. The Ulster words we used had to wait until the Troubles before being captured in print. I remember as a child being told that only people from our part of the world could pronounce the *gh* in 'lough' and 'sheugh' (ditch). When I first read Seamus Heaney's 'Broagh' in his 1972 volume, *Wintering Out*, I recognized what I'd been told as a child in the poem's closing lines:

> like that last
> *gh* the strangers found
> difficult to manage
> (Heaney 1980: 66)

Later, reading Paul Muldoon's 'Quoof', the title-poem of his 1983 volume, I saw that 'quoof', the Muldoons' 'family word/for the hot water bottle', is like one of those words we used inside our extended Ulster family. I say it is 'like' those words because I'm nearly sure Muldoon invented it, and he wants 'spoof' to be one of its meanings. A friend in Belfast says 'you're spoofing me', when he means you're lying or exaggerating. Discussing the poem in a reading he gave at the University of Arizona Poetry Center in 2002, Muldoon draws attention to this playful, cheeky sense of etymology:

For a long time I wondered if this might be a corruption of an Elizabethan word for a hot water bottle because there are of course such fossilizations in northern Ireland from the Elizabethan plantation. [*Audience laughter.*] Perhaps not. [*Audience laughter.*] Then I wondered if it might be a fossilization of an old Gaelic word for a hot water bottle; also perhaps not. [*Audience laughter.*] A while after I'd written it I asked my father about this word and he told me that the first time he'd heard it was from us, the kids. [*Audience laughter.*] Because I just assumed it had been handed down from generation to generation. [*Audience laughter.*]

(Muldoon 2002)

But in the poem, it is the word's lack of shared public meaning, its lack of history that is important: Muldoon plays with the awkward novelty of a word that is intimate to him but strange outside his own family circle. When Muldoon says that the word 'quoof' is like a 'shy beast/that has yet to enter the language', he dramatizes what it means to make a closed, familial dialect part of printed public language, and this publication of a family word might serve to represent the coming into print of Irish English words over the last 30 years or so.

When I wrote *A New Look at the Language Question*, in 1983, there were no dictionaries of Irish English: because of this, the language lacked 'any institutional existence and so is impoverished as a literary medium'. It was back then 'a language without a lexicon, a language without form' (Paulin 1983: 60). Over the last thirty years, writing in the North of Ireland has brought into print words which previously belonged to demotic, local speech, to the vernacular. Words such as 'boke', 'bake', 'scaldy', 'Mucker'. Lexicographers have responded to this extension of the language by the introduction of rude, embarrassing, impolite words. Caroline Macafee's *Dictionary of Ulster Dialect* (1996), James Fenton's *The Hamely Tongue* (1995) and Terry Dolan's *Dictionary of Hiberno-English* (1998) all contain words which have only recently emerged into print.

Looking at the six dictionaries of Irish English on my shelves, I find a small blue notebook that contains the words I learnt in childhood and beyond. This is a small personal word hoard, which I'll work through alphabetically.

A

amadan   this comes from the Irish *amadán*, meaning fool

In Ireland, there is a great love of place and place names, though some place names take on a pejorative tone and expression: **Antrim** is one such place name, always, as I've heard it in the last 30 years, voiced with a disgusted, dismissive tone.

ate   eat (ate is used as present tense)

B

black bag   is a term I encountered at scout camp more than 40 years ago, when the mother of a fellow scout told the scout leader proudly that the boy's uncle 'carries the black bag'. She meant he was a doctor.

bake   as in 'shut your bake', meaning 'mouth'

baste   usually 'wee baste' to designate not one of the big, heavy bastards; more a low, sneaky fellow

banjaxed   'worn out, broken down', and has apparently entered slang in Britain

bap   'head'

barmbrack   sometimes pronounced 'barnbrack', is a fruit loaf

beaten docket   as in 'he's a beaten docket', means he's finished, he's a failure, he's quite exploded

beg   'bag, sack'. The word carries a particular fear for me because my grandmother in Belfast had a gardener called Herby, who spoke with a strong Belfast accent, lived in an old folks' home and spent the afternoons in the cinema to keep warm. I messed up one of the flower beds in my Granny's garden and Herby, to everyone's amusement, became angry and told me he'd 'put me in a beg' if I did that again.

bin lid   'a stupid person'

big lad   The phrase 'big lad' is used in Belfast by one very close friend to another, as in 'OK big lad, we'd better be heading'. A friend from Dublin uses it when we meet – he acquired it from a mutual friend who grew up in Belfast. It is usually accompanied by a curt nod and a serious expression which gives way to a grin. From the term, one can deduce that male bonding is strong in Belfast.

blatherskite   'someone who talks a lot of nonsense, superficial nonsense'

blow in   'someone who has recently joined a community'

bodge   'to botch something'

boke   'vomit'; a 'dry boke' is 'retching'

bold   used of a badly behaved child

bonefire   bonfire

boortree   a 'bower tree' which is an elder tree. It is used by Heaney in 'Broagh' and is also used by Tennyson in one of his dialect poems.

boul   a term of approbation and admiration – as in 'the boul Henry'

brock man   Strabane term for the man who use to collect 'brock' or vegetable rubbish which was fed to the pigs. His smelly lorry was a feature of life in the 1950s in our area where he was called 'the pig man'. The word comes from the Irish *broc* which means 'leavings'. The Old High German 'brochân', which means 'to break into bits' is also relevant.

bubble, didn't come up the Lagan in a   When I was a child and I wanted to say 'don't treat me as though I'm naïve', I'd use the Belfast expression and say 'd'ya think I came floating up the Lagan in a bubble'. The Lagan is the main river that flows through the city.

but   commonly used at the end of a sentence, as in 'there was no one there but.' Imogen in *Cymbeline* says 'I would have broke mine eyestrings, cracked them but' (I.iii.17).

bungalow   'a stupid person'

C

cat   'unpleasant', often used of a bad smell

catch yourself on   'get wise', 'stop being silly'. At the beginning of the Troubles, the distinguished theatre director Sir Tyrone Guthrie made a speech just before close-down on local television pleading with the population of Ulster not to go down the road of political and sectarian violence. He finished by saying 'as we say here, would you ever catch yourselves on'. Sadly, he was ignored.

champ   At primary school, it was always good when we got champ with our stew: mashed potatoes with chopped scallions – spring onions. The word 'scallion' comes from the French 'escalogne' and must have been brought to Ireland by the Normans. The word 'champ' is always voiced with glee and relish.

childer   In the North of Ireland, children are often referred to by the Middle English word 'childer', which has greater tenderness than 'children'.

clabber   soft sticky mud

cleg   a horse fly

combulsion   'a whole mixture'

could   'cold – i.e. very cold'

craychur   Of someone who is suffering and of whom one is fond and sorry for one might say 'the craychur!' This is similar to the expression 'the poor sawl'.

Cullybackey   a triumphal place name always pronounced with a shout as 'CullyBACKY!'

cunty hooks   an endearment

D

dead spit   I remember when I first heard the phrase 'dead spit'. At primary school, there was a girl I always thought of with great respect, partly because she had a very unusual first name – Ingela. She was called Ingela Dixon. One day my friend Neill pointed to a girl outside the school and said 'she's the dead spit of Ingela'. I remember thinking how ugly the phrase 'dead spit' was compared with the music of Ingela, though it is more concrete and imaginative than 'exact resemblance'.

dekko, take a   to take a look

docken   'dock leaves', an Old English plural form (again it is used by Heaney in 'Broagh')

dote   is used, often in 'a wee dote', of an attractive small child. An especially lovable grown-up might be called a 'dote'.

doughhead   'a stupid person'

dummy tit   is a child's comforter

duncher   a cloth cap

dwammy   is used to describe someone with a dozy manner

E

eejit   an 'idiot', but the term is gentler

exacktly!   In conversation, when two people from the North of Ireland arrive at the same idea simultaneously they shout out 'Exacktly!'

F

feck   softer version 'fuck'

filum   'film' (often jocose)

footless   to be drunk

footer   to fiddle about uselessly with work that doesn't get done

for   used sometimes with a conscious heaviness and gaucheness, as in 'I want for to check something'. Also used to mean 'because', as in 'I didn't want to go there, for it was a wick wee place'.

fornenst   'next to', as in this greatly loved Belfast street song:

> My Aunt Jane she's awful smart
> she bakes wee rings in an apple tart
> and when Halloween comes round
> fornenst that tart I'm always found
> and when Halloween comes round
> fornenst that tart I'm always found.
> ('My Aunt Jane')

full shilling, not the   a person whose personality doesn't quite add up is sometimes described as 'not the full shilling'

fuzzy-wuzzy colony   In 1971, the Lord Mayor of Belfast, Alderman Cairns, complained that the then Northern Ireland home secretary was treating Northern Ireland like such a colony.

G

ganch   a 'fool, a simpleton', I think a heavily built fool

geg   someone who is good fun to be with, or it is a social occasion like a gate-crashed party where good but slightly risky fun has been had

get   'a bastard, an unpleasant person'

girn   'to complain', used of children whining

glype   'a fool'

gobshite   someone who talks bullshit

good on you towney   'well done, well spoken' – in the sense of having spoken up for a cause

grip   'a soft bag'

gunk   'a snub, a blow, a rebuff'. As in 'a quare gunk'.

H

halves, go   'to split something'

hallion   'an irresponsible person'

hames, make a   'make a mess of something'

hare sit, let the   'to leave some issue where it is in case it is politically risky to raise it'

header   'someone who takes too many risks'

hoke   'to dig, pull something, say, from under a rock'

hoor   'whore'

hoult, take a   'take a hold'

hows about ye?   'how are you keeping?'

howsomever   'however'

I

ignorant   'grossly bad-mannered and tactless'

IT!   children mocking another child who is dressed differently cry out 'would you look at IT!'

J

japped   water splashed on a surface, say round a sink is 'japped'

jeuk   to dodge around people and obstacles is to 'jeuk'

K

kilter, out of   'out of line, wrong'

L

Larne   like Antrim a pejorative place name. As in the response to a complaint about how depressing things are: 'were you ever in Larne on a wet day?'

long may your lum reek   'long may your chimney smoke', an expression of admiration at success

lumbering   used of adolescents kissing and cuddling vigorously in 1960s Belfast

lunkhead 'a dopey, thick person'. In Traynor's *The English Dialect of Donegal*, 'lunk' is defined as '1. *adj.* Of a day: close, sultry. It's a terrible lunk heat the day; [cf. Norw. dial. *lunke*, tepid degree of heat.] 2. *adv.* Having a sickly feeling. I was feeling lunk. [App. Don. only.]'

M

make, hasn't a 'hasn't a penny'
manky 'gone off, unpleasant'
marley 'marble'
milly a mill girl. Once a common sight on the streets of Belfast, they often walked arm in arm, scarves covering their hair, which was usually in curlers. They laughed and smoked and were rumoured to practice humiliating initiation rites on young men when they joined a factory. They wore short skirts, smoked Woodbine or Park Drive and were always laughing and joking.
mitch 'play truant'. Hamlet speaks of 'miching mallecho' (III.ii) and Falstaff asks if the sun will 'prove a micher and eat blackberries' (*1 Henry IV*, II.iv).
mischeeveeous 'mischievous'
murials murals in working-class areas are called 'murials'

N

nae bother 'no bother'
night is set, the 'it is night'
nurration, kick up a 'kick up a fuss'

O

ould 'old'
our used to identify a child, as in 'our Jimmy'

P

pachle 'a heap', used of a lazy, slovenly, demoralized person
parlatic 'to be very drunk'. Synonyms are: poleaxed, jarred, puddled, punctured, paladic, plucked, blocked, blitzed, snattered, stocious, steamboats, elephantsed, arsified, blootered, lockjawed, full. To be quietly drunk is to be 'happy'.
piece 'a piece of buttered bread, sometimes with jam on it'. When I was a child, I'd call with some friends on a nice old couple down the street. We'd knock on the door and say 'would you give us a piece!' The old woman would go to the kitchen and return with a plate on which were slices of buttered bread sprinkled with sugar. To ask for a piece is to return to the language of childhood.

picture/pixture   to call someone a 'picture' is to say they are a sight
pooley, make   'urinate'
Portiedown   is a way of referring slightly pejoratively to Portadown, a notoriously loyalist town
pranye, she'll have a   'she'll have a fit'
pumpture   'a puncture'

R

ridiklus   'ridiculous', as in 'what he said was absolutely ridiklus'
right there, you're   a polite way of pretending to agree with someone who has said something stupid or with which you disagree. A less hearty, but equally diplomatic and insincere, alternative is 'I see what you're saying'. In management theory this is called 'the mirror technique'.
roast   'to blush'. Alternative, 'to hit a reddener'.

S

scaldy   When a small boy had an especially short haircut we would gather round and shout 'scaldy!' A scaldy is a tiny fledgling, first hatched (the word goes back to the Old Norse word for 'bald').
scrake of dawn   'the crack of dawn', the word refers to the dawn chorus
scunner, take a   'to take a dislike to'
shut the fuck up   'would you really shut up now'
skelf   'a little splinter in one's foot, finger or hand'
skinnymalink   'a tall, thin person', usually said admiringly and fondly to a small child. It is a term of endearment.
so there you are now   a common filler after an anecdote has ended
soda heads   racist term for protestants used in Strabane
spalpeen   'fool'. I learnt it from Ian Paisley, who was interviewed on radio by a journalist many years ago. He asked him his reaction to a remark by Jeffrey Archer that he, Paisley, would make an excellent president of a United Ireland. Paisley retorted that this reminded him of a moment when Daniel O'Connell was accused of something that was patently untrue and he replied 'the man that said that is a spalpeen'. Paisley's speeches and sermons can be discussed under the rubric 'Rude'. Many years ago he described Unionists as puppet politicians who 'are but grasshoppers with portfolios'. He also described the Swiss, after they refused to let a plane he was on land at Geneva (he wanted to protest against the Pope), as 'a nation of dimwits whose only contribution to the twentieth century has been the cuckoo clock'. This is Dr Paisley's account of his meeting with Mr Major:

'When we entered the room Mr Major said to me: "Except you now give me a categorical assurance that you believe me, I will not talk with you." I told

Mr Major: "When you hear my submission, you will know what my position is."

Mr Major: "I will not listen to your submission, except you right now give me a categorical assurance that you believe my word."

Mr Paisley: "You are the first Prime Minister that ever asked a political opponent in this room, or outside this room, that if he doesn't swear he believes in your truthfulness, then you will not listen to him."

He said: "Get out of this room and never come back until you are prepared to say that I speak the truth and do not tell lies." '

(Laird 1999: xii)

Sir Patrick Mayhew's account

Sir Patrick said Mr Major saw no purpose in answering Mr Paisley's questions if he declined to accept the word of the British Prime Minister [that there had been no secret deal with the IRA]. The Prime Minister invited the DUP leader from the outset to say whether he accepted his word:

'Dr Paisley declined to answer that question. The Prime Minister reiterated it. Dr Paisley said that would become clear in the course of a submission he wished to make.

The Prime Minister heard the submission and reiterated the question.

The answer was not forthcoming so the Prime Minister said he saw no purpose whatsoever in answering the questions Dr Paisley had put.'

(Laird 1999: xiii)

There is an extensive analysis of these two versions in Laird 1999. Commenting on Paisley's account, Andrew Laird notes that ' "Except you now" is an Irish idiom – in English "unless" would be used instead of "except" '. Yet Paisley, he notes, 'twice attributes the use of this Irish idiom to Major, who is English' (1999: 220). Laird also discusses the room for manoeuvre which Patrick Mayhew's use of indirect discourse has over Paisley's use of direct discourse. Mayhew uses what we might term proper, civil speech – uses it cunningly – while Paisley uses much more vivid and emotional speech, but speech which will not allow for compromise or consensus.

starved   very cold

T

tay 'tea'
the which 'which' (emphatic), as in 'I lent him a book, the which I never saw again'
thrawn someone who is 'thrawn' or 'thran' is both stubborn and clumsy
titter of wit, have a 'catch yourself on'

toty   'tiny', as in a 'toty wee thing'. It is always used affectionately.

throughother   used of, say, an untidy room, an adjective used by Hopkins in 'Spelt from Sibyll's Leaves':

> as-
> tray or aswarm, all throughther, in throngs; | self ín self steepèd and páshed
> – qúite
> Disremembering.

(Hopkins 1967: 97)

The word comes from the Irish *trína chéile*, meaning 'mixed up, confused'. Hopkins also uses an Irish English word for forget – 'disremember'.

W

wee buns   'easy'. The word 'wee' is a favourite – as in 'my own wee man', spoken to a baby or young child as a term of deep endearment. A 'wee doll' is a cheeky, sexist term employed by a young man passing a young woman in the street, usually when he's in the company of other young men and wanting to sound a note of bravado. A 'wee man' otherwise is a not very gifted person in a position of authority he should not hold. A 'wee phone' – as in 'I'll give you a wee phone' – is a phone call which I'll make sometime, but which you shouldn't worry about or think of as urgent or important.

well done yourself   a term of praise

whin   'gorse'

wheen   'a large number'

wick   'unpleasant and useless'

wind dog   'a fragment of a rainbow'

windies   'windows'

Y

It is common to use 'ye' for 'you' and 'yous' as the plural.

yo   a ewe

Looking through my various dictionaries, I realize that Ulster speech contains many more words than the few I've given above. These are the words and expressions I still use in everyday speech, and sometimes when I write. They all have for me a certain éclat and energy, as well as sometimes a tenderness and gentleness which is part of their orality, part of their blunt, monosyllabic, you could say rudeness, if that word were to be redefined and had its pejorative sting removed. These rude words map out familial bonds, but they can also convey a sense of intimacy and familiarity to those for whom they are not part of everyday speech. To include them in dictionaries of standard English is to broaden the emotional as well as the social and geographical range of the language. I now dream of a very capacious dictionary, which contains all the words used on the island. It should contain the word *roti*, the Punjabi word for chapatti, a word I've always heard spoken in a Strabane accent and which is one of those words like *piece* that make me feel at home. But I know that a truly eloquent, civil language has to rise beyond any possible accusations of rudeness, tribalism, localism. If I'd stayed in Leeds I might have come to that conclusion sooner – or I might not.

Bibliography

Dolan, T. P. (ed.) (1998) *A Dictionary of Hiberno-English: The Irish Use of English*, Dublin: Gill & Macmillan.

Fenton, J. (ed.) (1995) *The Hamely Tongue: A Personal Record of Ulster-Scots in County Antrim*, Newtownards: Ulster-Scots Academic Press.

Heaney, S. (1980) *Selected Poems, 1965–1975*, London: Faber and Faber.

Hopkins, G. M. (1955) *The Correspondence of Gerard Manly Hopkins and Richard Watson Dixon*, ed. C. C. Abbott, 2nd rev. edn, London: Oxford University Press; repr. 1970.

—— (1967) *The Poems of Gerard Manley Hopkins*, ed. W. H. Gardner and N. H. Mackenzie, 4th edn, London: Oxford University Press.

Laird, A. (1999) *Powers of Expression, Expressions of Power: Speech Presentation and Latin Literature*, Oxford: Oxford University Press.

Macafee, C. I. (ed.) (1996) *A Concise Ulster Dictionary*, Oxford: Oxford University Press.

Muldoon, P. (1996) *New Selected Poems, 1968–1994*, London: Faber and Faber.

—— (2002) transcription of Paul Muldoon reading from his work: University of Arizona Poetry Center, Visiting Poets and Writers Reading Series, 30 January 2002, available online at <http://www.paulmuldoon.net/recordings.php4> (accessed November 2006).

O Muirithe, D. (1996) *A Dictionary of Anglo-Irish: Words and Phrases from Gaelic in the English of Ireland*, Blackrock: Four Courts Press.

Paulin, T. (1983) 'A New Look at the Language Question', in *Writing to the Moment: Selected Critical Essays, 1980–1996*, London: Faber and Faber, 1996.

Robinson, P. (1997) *Ulster-Scots: A Grammar of the Traditional Written and Spoken Language*, Belfast: Ullans Press.

Share, B. (ed.) (1997) *Slanguage: A Dictionary of Slang and Colloquial English in Ireland*, Dublin: Gill & Macmillan.

Traynor, M. (1953) *The English Dialect of Donegal: A Glossary Incorporating the Collections of H. C. Hart*, Dublin: Royal Irish Academy.

Part II

British bawdy

Chapter 5

Orwell's dirty postcards

David Pascoe

In the late summer of 1947, the novelist Anthony Powell sent a picture postcard to his friend and fellow Etonian, George Orwell, then rehabilitating at Barnhill on the Isle of Jura. Shortly afterwards, Orwell responded with a long letter, describing his daily routine on the unexpectedly bedroughted island, which began: 'Thanks so much for your postcard which I think was rather lucky to get here – at any rate I think the crofter who brings the post the last seven miles might have suppressed it if he had seen it' (Orwell 1998, vol. 19: 200).

Mischievously, Powell had sent an example of what Orwell had publicly described six years earlier as one of those ' "comics" of the cheap stationers' windows, the penny or twopenny coloured post cards', so easily recognizable by 'their crude drawing and unbearable colours, chiefly hedge-sparrow's egg tint and Post Office red', and signed with the monicker 'Donald McGill' (Orwell 1998, vol. 13: 23). The card he had selected (Figure 5.1) – a classic of its kind – depicts a scene in a newsagent's shop, whose look Orwell described at length in his essay on 'Boys' Weeklies', published in *Horizon* in early 1940:

> The general appearance of these shops is always very much the same: a few posters for the *Daily Mail* and the *News of the World* outside, a poky little window with sweet-bottles and packets of Players, and a dark interior smelling of liquorice allsorts and festooned from floor to ceiling with vilely printed twopenny papers, most of them with lurid cover-illustrations in three colours.
>
> (Orwell 1998, vol. 12: 57–8)

Orwell concludes his description by observing that that 'the contents of these shops is the best available indication of what the mass of the English people really feels and thinks' (Orwell 1998, vol. 12: 58). For, as well as these papers, newsagents – particularly those in Northern resorts – would shift huge numbers of the card which Powell despatched to the Inner Hebrides. Behind the counter, under the sign for the small lending library most such shops contained, stands a bright-eyed bare-shouldered young woman in half profile, her hair immaculately Marcel waved, and her hand cocked confidently on her hip. Her outfit is

" Do you keep stationery, Miss ? "
" Well, I wriggle about a bit, sometimes ! "

Figure 5.1 Postcard by McGill, c. 1940.

striking: polka-dotted and plunge-necked, it might easily be the top half of a swimming costume of a style popular on more open-minded British beaches between the wars. She looks directly at a young man standing the other side of the counter. His head, in profile, is wonderfully chinless; his nose is upturned and his hat too small for his skull. The edge of the worktop, on which he rests his kid-gloved right hand, is exactly level with his groin; his legs are slightly bent, and he seems to be leaning into the wood. His left arm is bent at the elbow so that his other hand is invisible, but it's possible that it's in his trouser pocket, fumbling and fondling the small change for his potential purchase. An advertisement for the day's *Daily Howl* stands propped against the counter and it announces 'Runners and Betting', for the benefit of studiers of form, such as he. The caption, printed starkly above the image, runs as follows: *Male Customer*: 'Do you keep stationery, Miss?' *Young Lady Assistant*: 'Well, I wriggle about a bit, sometimes!' Little wonder that Orwell was surprised at the GPO's safe delivery of the card to his lodgings on the strictly Free Presbyterian island, since the relation between image and word has here created a startlingly unexpected *double entendre*, raising questions not just of the nitty gritty of sexual technique, but also suggesting that the young woman knows exactly what this male customer is really asking for as he looks at her; and it is not a ream of paper.

Clearly, in posting off this card to Jura, Powell was, in part, indulging Orwell's passionate interest in what, since 1947, has been known as deltiology, a hobby begun at prep school, developed at Eton and refined still further during trips to the Continent.[1] Memories of that last stage emerge in remarks made in 1944, when he claimed that 'some of Dali's pictures would tend to poison the imagination like a pornographic postcard'; namely, those 'dirty postcards that used to be sold in Mediterranean seaport towns', and no doubt picked up by travellers, like venereal diseases, willy-nilly (Orwell 1998, vol. 16: 236, 238). In the French capital, though, the connoisseur might not always get what he paid for, as Orwell recalls the sharp practices of Rougiers, 'an old ragged, dwarfish couple who plied an extraordinary trade' on the Boulevard St Michel, selling a highly sought-after form of stationery: the postcard. 'The curious thing was that the postcards were sold in sealed packets as pornographic ones, but were actually photographs of châteaux on the Loire; the buyers did not discover this till too late, and of course never complained' (Orwell 1998, vol. 1: 3). That 'of course' perhaps carries a deal of experience; a lifetime of keeping stationery under wraps. Bernard Crick claims that, when at prep school at St Cyprian's, Orwell 'collected in an album seaside picture-postcards purchased at Eastbourne, largely of ladies with big bottoms; but he also had a manilla envelope with cards judged too vulgar' to be shown in mixed company (Crick 1992: 91). Another biography – the 'Authorised' version, allegedly – claims that, in fact, penny postcards containing 'illustrations of big-breasted women in tight dresses' were most appealing to Orwell, and that, furthermore, 'By the time he was in his forties, he had collected hundreds of them and kept them in a large drawer' (Shelden 1991: 70). However, in contrast to Auden's locating of Housman's tears kept in a drawer 'like dirty postcards', Orwell's fondness for such stationery was frequently made public (Auden 1977: 238). Of 'comic coloured postcards, especially Donald McGill's' he admitted to Desmond Hawkins on a live radio broadcast in December 1940, that 'I'm particularly attached to those' (Orwell 1998, vol. 12: 298). Later, the arguments in favour of this form of pictorial culture were enveloped in the unsealed and open-ended dimensions of a justly famous essay, first published in *Horizon* in September 1941.

On its first appearance, 'The Art of Donald McGill' was furnished by reproductions of two of McGill's cards, possibly loaned to Connolly by Orwell.[2] In one, an obese spiv, accompanied by a strikingly full-figured young woman, is depicted telling a hotel receptionist, 'I and my daughter would like adjoining bedrooms!'; in the other, a speaker advocating temperance from his soap-box concludes his oration with 'Now I have just one tract left. What shall I do with it?' Nearby, a wife is shown with her hand over her portly husband's mouth, preventing him responding, with the caption: 'Don't say it George.' But in his essay George Orwell did, in fact, 'say' the unsayable about this fundamental form of English popular culture; and in such terms that Alex Comfort, whose pacifist novel Orwell had treated to a hostile review earlier in the year, wrote to tell him that the article on McGill 'was the best example of an analysis I think I ever read' (Orwell 1998, vol. 13: 406).

Orwell opens his account by admitting 'Who Donald McGill is, I do not know. He is apparently a trade name . . . but he is unquestionably a real person with a style of drawing which is recognizable at a glance' (Orwell 1998, vol. 13: 23–4). In fact, the real McGill was born in London in 1875 and died in 1962 in Blackheath, where he spent most of his life after he lost a foot in a school rugby incident. His career in draughtsmanship began in 1904 after he sent an illustrated card to a sick nephew; his brother-in-law was highly impressed and suggested that McGill undertake it professionally. Within a year, graphic art had become his full-time occupation, and over the next half century, more than 350 million of his cards were sold. His most famous design, one which no doubt particularly appealed to Orwell, shifted six million copies. It depicted a young couple, sitting in the shade of a tree. High-mindedly, the man asks his companion: 'Do you like Kipling?' The woman replies promptly: 'I don't know, you naughty boy; I've never kippled.' Designs such as this would lead to financial security for McGill's publishers, if not for the artist himself, who was paid no royalty, but only a flat fee for each design; and the draughtsmanship would also lead to a degree of notoriety for McGill and, eventually, to his prosecution for obscenity.[3]

In a recent elegy on the seaside postcard, D. J. Taylor has claimed: 'The appeal of these rectangles of flaring, badly drawn smut lay almost entirely in their air of licensed subversion: the fact that they were on public display and that no real power existed that could stop you looking at them' (Taylor 2001). Orwell, however, was more realistic, pointing out that 'Newsagents are occasionally prosecuted for selling them, and there would be many more prosecutions if the broadest jokes were not invariably protected by double meanings' (Orwell 1998, vol. 13: 28). By the time the Tories returned to power in 1951, the year after Orwell's death, the *double entendres* were being single-mindedly read by self-appointed 'Watch Committees' in seaside towns who, in due course, prohibited dozens of McGill's postcards. In 1953, Brighton ordered 113 of his designs to be destroyed; Weymouth destroyed 2,000 cards; while uniquely, Eastbourne, the town where Orwell began his own postcard collection, banned McGill outright. The same year, newsagents and fancy goods emporia in Cleethorpes were raided by the police, who confiscated bundles of McGill's postcards, including one depicting a small man on a beach, surrounded by bathing beauties, who is balancing a large stick of rock on his groin, with the caption 'A stick of rock, cock?' (see Figure 5.2) In the face of this evidence, the Director of Public Prosecutions agreed that the chief constable of Lincolnshire should bring a prosecution at the Lincoln Quarter Session in July 1954 under the Obscene Publications Act of 1857. McGill prepared a suitably stiff defence against the charge: 'I was amazed when a double meaning was pointed out to me after publication only . . . the word cock was put in as it rhymed and was [a] very popular and ordinary word of cockney greeting. From the drawing it is perfectly obvious that the man is taking the weight just above his knees. The ends of the wrapping paper show this clearly' (cited in Kennedy 2004). However, on the day of the trial, McGill followed the advice of his lawyer and

Figure 5.2 Postcard by McGill, c. 1950.

pleaded guilty and was fined £50 with court costs of £25, plus his own substantial legal costs. As a result of the case, the postcard industry shrank; retailers, fearful of the police raiding their premises, cancelled orders, and several of the smaller companies were wound up.

However, when Orwell's essay was published just over a decade earlier, McGill's designs were both 'completely typical', the very 'norm of the comic postcard', and ubiquitously popular – in 1939, a million copies of McGill's cards were sold in Blackpool alone. (But then, as Orwell once observed, 'Blackpool is more typical than Ascot' (Orwell 1998, vol. 16: 200).) Orwell, the connoisseur, is frank about the appearance of the cards: one's 'first impression is of overwhelming vulgarity. This is quite apart from the ever-present obscenity, and apart from the hideousness of the colours. They have an utter lowness of mental atmosphere which comes out not only in the nature of the jokes but, even more, in the grotesque, staring, blatant quality of the drawings . . . full of heavy lines and empty spaces' (Orwell 1998, vol. 13: 24). But, as he lays out the 'typical' themes of these cards, his second thought is quite distinct, and amounts to 'indefinable familiarity'. The roster of subject matter runs as follows: 'sex jokes, ranging from the harmless to the all but unprintable'; 'home life', as experienced by 'the henpecked husband'; drunkenness, which is '*ipso facto* funny'; W.C.'s, since 'Chamberpots are *ipso facto* funny, and so are public lavatories'; inter-working-class snobbery, where 'the "swell" is almost as automatically a figure of fun as the slum-dweller'; stock figures, such as the Scotsman ('almost inexhaustible'), the swindling lawyer, the bumbling clergyman, the ' "knut" or "masher" ' in dated evening attire, sometimes 'even with spats and a knobby cane'; and finally, politics, notwithstanding the fact that the cards never 'attempt to induce an outlook acceptable to the ruling class' (Orwell 1998, vol. 13: 25–6).

Michael Shelden has described Orwell's account as 'an argument in favour of those claims on our attention which we are tempted to dismiss as useless, trivial, and even faintly absurd' (Shelden 1991: 389). This is altogether too innocent, since, as the essay continues, it becomes a defence – indeed, a celebration – of what Orwell describes as 'the outstanding, all-important feature of comic post cards – their obscenity' (Orwell 1998, vol. 13: 26). During the last decade of his life, Orwell would make several attempts to come to terms with obscenity. In the famously brilliant account of Henry Miller that forms the first section of 'Inside the Whale', for instance, he notes that he writes 'about the man in the street, and it is incidentally rather a pity that it should be a street full of brothels'; somehow, the obscenity gets in the way of Miller's distinctive 'flowing, swelling prose, a prose with rhythms in it', even though, in the case of *Tropic of Cancer*, it was 'only natural that the first thing people notice should be its obscenity' (Orwell 1998, vol. 12: 88, 89). Orwell continues:

> Given our current notions of literary decency, it is not at all easy to
> approach an unprintable book with detachment. Either one is shocked

and disgusted, or one is morbidly thrilled, or one is determined above all not to be impressed. The last is probably the commonest reaction, with the result that unprintable books often get less attention than they deserve.

(Orwell 1998, vol. 12: 89)

Hence the instinct – for the mid-century Englishman at least – is to look away at the point of nausea. In his essay on Dali, written in 1944 for the *Saturday Book*, and itself suppressed on the grounds of obscenity by Hutchinson, its unnerved publishers, Orwell observed: 'Obscenity is a very difficult question to discuss honestly. People are too frightened either of seeming to be shocked or of seeming not to be shocked, to be able to define the relationship between art and morals' (Orwell 1998, vol. 16: 237). In the case of Dali, Orwell was fearless in his exposure of the Spaniard's sensations; nothing other than 'a symptom of the world's illness' (Orwell 1998, vol. 16: 238). Yet behind the erotic and fetishistic frissons, the necrophilia and coprophagy, the artist's graphic style reminded Orwell of little more than Edwardian picturesque, the kitsch feudal worlds of Barrie, Rackham, and Dunsany; exactly the worlds against which McGill's luridly sociable draughtsmanship reacted so strongly. Most of all, though, Orwell's account of Dali objected to the Spanish artist being given the benefit of clergy; that is, exempted from 'the moral laws that are binding on ordinary people' (Orwell 1998, vol. 16: 237).

By contrast, Donald McGill's art 'only has meaning in relation to a fairly strict moral code', and strictly applied to the masses; namely the institution of marriage, and the four leading jokes contained therein: 'nakedness, illegitimate babies, old maids and newly married couples', none of which, adds Orwell, would seem to be amusing in a 'dissolute or even "sophisticated" society' (Orwell 1998, vol. 13: 27). However, England between the wars was anything but; it was, as he observed in February 1941, a nation gifted neither artistically nor intellectually, whose 'crowds in the big towns, with their mild knobby faces, their bad teeth and gentle manners, are different from a European crowd' (Orwell 1998, vol. 12: 392). As ever, Orwell returns to the caricature, the form of depiction which he so valued in McGill's art, and at the heart of which lay responsible relief; in effect, it blew 'a chorus of raspberries' in the face of those high-minded sentiments uttered by politicians, clergy and the like (Orwell 1998, vol. 13: 29).

At that time, early in the war, Orwell was still optimistic enough to believe that when circumstances demanded, 'human beings are heroic'; however, we can't all be heroes all of the time, and so, naturally, that other element, 'the lazy, cowardly, debt-bilking adulterer who is inside all of us, can never be suppressed altogether' (Orwell 1998, vol. 13: 29, 30). Orwell's essay is happy to identify the figure who epitomizes such a 'view of life' (Orwell 1998, vol. 13: 28): Cervantes's Sancho Panza, the sidekick of the high-minded but dim-witted Don Quixote, is the ultimate embodiment of 'real *lowness*' (Orwell 1998, vol. 12: 253). He is 'your unofficial self, the voice of the belly protesting against the soul', his tastes pointing in the direction of 'safety, soft beds, no work, pots of beer and women with "voluptuous" figures'. A few years later, W. H. Auden put it more abstractly: 'Sancho Panza is a realist in that it is always the actual world, the immediate moment, which he enjoys, not an imaginary world or an anticipated future, but a "holy" realist in that he enjoys the actual and immediate for its own sake, not for any material satisfactions it provides' (Auden 1963: 137). Hence Panza meets and moulds the fact 'human beings want to be good, but not too good, and not quite all the time'; and this permits Orwell to ask a pertinent question of his readership: 'If you look into your own mind, which are you, Don Quixote or Sancho Panza? Almost certainly you are both' (Orwell 1998, vol. 12: 30, 29). As John Coleman has observed of Orwell: 'He was a trustworthy writer, *un type sérieux*, and he said it was perfectly all right to enjoy manifestations of low art. He steadily visited the part of us which he described as "Sancho Panza" – that lazing *alter ego*, somnolent in the bath, or "too tired to go to bed" – and came back with encouraging reports. But it was the "Don Quixote" who produced the reports' (Coleman 1971: 103–4). Hence, viewed in this light, Powell's postcard seems even more acutely chosen, and might even come to represent Orwell in the stationer's shop, standing tall before the counter; the Don, as it were, faced with the raw materials of his work, here overseen by a female Panza in polka dots.

In his review of *Applesauce* – a variety show staged at the Holborn Empire in September 1940 featuring the 'cheeky chappy' Max Miller – Orwell observed that 'so long as comedians like Max Miller are on the stage and the comic coloured postcards which express approximately the same view of life are in the stationers' windows, one knows that the popular culture of England is surviving' (Orwell 1998, vol. 12: 253). Analysing the comedian's act, Orwell noted that Miller, resembling 'a Middlesex Street hawker' in his 'tail coat and shiny top hat', was the latest in 'a long line of English comedians who have specialized in the Sancho Panza side of life', the expression of which 'needs more talent than to express nobility'. The comedian's 'startling obscenities . . . are only possible because they are expressed in *doubles entendres* which imply a common background in the audience'. The *double entendre* turns on a disjunction; its key movement is pivotal, in every respect, in that the second meaning dwells on the working-class stereotype lying behind that adjective, 'common'. Hence the popularity of the combination of word and image, the *double entendre* typified by McGill's style, is 'symptomatically important': 'Like the music halls, [the postcards] are a sort of saturnalia, a harmless rebellion against virtue' (Orwell 1998, vol. 13: 30). At this point in his essay on McGill, Orwell turns away from the pile of cards to the Bible, and for his labours now frames the draughtsmanship with Ecclesiastes 7.15–17 instead, chapter and verse:

> there is a just man that perishes in his righteousness, and there is a wicked man that prolongeth his life in his wickedness. Be not righteous over much; neither make thyself over wise; why shouldst thou destroy thyself? Be not

overmuch wicked, neither be though foolish: why shouldest thou die before thy time?

The advice bears the virtue of Solomon's pragmatism and, directed towards McGill's practice, it allows him the ultimate leeway of the *double entendre*; not the benefit of clergy, but the benefit of doubt.

In an essay, 'Funny, But Not Vulgar', written in December 1944, Orwell maintained that 'The great age of English humorous writing – not witty and not satrirical, but simply humorous – was the first three-quarters of the nineteenth century' a period which saw, among other notable achievements, 'Dickens's enormous output of comic writings, Thackeray's brilliant burlesques' flourish alongside the 'comic draughtsmanship' of 'Cruickshank's illustrations of Dickens, and even Thackeray's illustrations of his own work' (Orwell 1998, vol. 16: 482–3). Yet, three years earlier, the conclusion of his account of McGill's art had stiffened into a lament that a 'whole category of humour, integral to our literature till 1800 or thereabouts, has dwindled down to these ill-drawn post cards, leading a barely legal existence' (Orwell 1998, vol. 13: 30). Such expressions of the waxing and waning of national comic traditions would become a common theme of Orwell's wartime criticism, but in 1941 it is linked to his sense that obscenity was being too strictly policed: tracked down, and forced to march into a *cordon sanitaire*. (The postcard would survive, no doubt, but it would be denuded of its imagery, to emerge in *Nineteen Eighty-Four* (1949) as little more than a means of communication: 'For the messages that it was occasionally necessary to send, there were printed postcards with long lists of phrases, and you struck out the ones that were inapplicable' (Orwell 1998, vol. 9: 116).) His essay 'Funny, but not Vulgar' laments the current state of verbal comedy: 'If you want a laugh you are likelier to go to a music-hall or a Disney film, or switch on Tommy Handley, or buy a few of Donald McGill's postcards, than to resort to a book or a periodical' (Orwell 1998, vol. 16: 483). What Orwell derides as the 'silly-ass tradition' paralysing modern British humour, is exemplified by A. P. Herbert's verse or P. G. Wodehouse's prose, 'aimed at prosperous stockbrokers whiling away an odd half hour in the lounge of some suburban golf course', and characterized by 'the avoidance of brutality and horror of intelligence'. Such a trend could only be summed up in the phrase '*funny without being vulgar*'. But Orwell retouches his definition: ' "Vulgar" in this context usually means "obscene," and it can be admitted at once that the best jokes are not necessarily dirty ones.' Nevertheless, he regards the contemporary emphasis on what is called clean fun as nothing other than 'the symptom of a general unwillingness to touch upon any serious or controversial subject' (Orwell 1998, vol. 16: 483–4):

> Obscenity is, after all, a kind of subversiveness. Chaucer's 'Miller's Tale' is a rebellion in the moral sphere, as *Gulliver's Travels* is a rebellion in the political sphere. The truth is that you cannot be memorably funny without

at some point raising topics which the rich, the powerful and the complacent would prefer to see left alone.

(Orwell 1998, vol. 16: 484)

Hence, in Chaucer's hands, Nicholas's crude wooing of Alysoun leaves something to *double entendre*, but most to desire: 'prively he caughte her by the queynte / And seyde, "Ywis, but if ich have my wille, / For deerne love of thee, lemman, I spille" ' (Chaucer 1988: 69). 'Wille' may announce the intention to act, but rhymed with 'spille', the exact nature of the act is made rather more explicit, directed as it is towards Alysoun's 'queynte'. In Lilliput, Gulliver's public micturition on the seat of a conflagration at the Palace has the result that 'in three Minutes the Fire was wholly extinguished; and the rest of that Noble Pile, which had cost so many Ages in erecting, preserved from Destruction' (Swift 1998: 43). In each case, there is a sense of the inherent fragility at the heart of institutions, be it the sanctity of marriage or the permanence of the nobility.

And McGill's cards, too, reflected a rebellion in the face of authority, even if their good faith meant risking charges of obscenity, and in consequence, suppression in the public interest. For, as Orwell notes, in England of the mid-twentieth century, it was not only sex that was 'vulgar': 'So are death, childbirth and poverty, the other three subjects upon which the best music-hall humour turns. [. . .] You cannot be really funny if your main aim is to flatter the comfortable classes: it means leaving out too much. To be funny, indeed, you have got to be serious' (Orwell 1998, vol. 16: 486). Orwell's own peculiar seriousness of purpose was often mistaken for gallows humour, but the corollary of this position was compelling: for him to have taken McGill as seriously as he did, the draughtsman must have proved that his 'vulgar and ugly' illustrations of 'mental rebellion, a momentary wish that things were otherwise', were more than just 'funny' (Orwell 1998, vol. 13: 29). In effect, as Orwell's fine essays suggest, they were the barest of a nation's necessities.

Notes

1 The *OED*'s first citation of *deltiology* – the hobby of collecting postcards – is drawn from the *New York Times* in June 1947. The word is derived from the Greek for 'writing tablet', δελτοσ.
2 Bernard Crick has suggested that 'He may have still had this collection in 1941 when he wrote "The Art of Donald McGill" '(Crick 1992: 91).
3 My account of McGill's life and work is indebted to Calder-Marshall 1966 and Buckland 1984.

References

Auden, W. H. (1963) *The Dyer's Hand*, London: Faber and Faber.
—— (1977) *The English Auden*, ed. E. Mendelson, London: Faber and Faber.

Buckland, E. (1984) *The World of Donald McGill*, Poole: Javelin.

Calder-Marshall, A. (1966) *Wish You Were Here: The Art of Donald McGill*, London: Hutchinson.

Chaucer, G. (1988) *The Riverside Chaucer*, ed. L. D. Benson, 3rd edn, Oxford: Oxford University Press.

Coleman, J. (1971) 'The Critic of Popular Culture', in M. Gross (ed.) *The World of George Orwell*, London: Weidenfeld and Nicolson, pp. 101–11.

Crick, B. (1992) *George Orwell: A Life*, new edn, London: Penguin.

Kennedy, M. (2004) 'Exhibition Marks 50 Years of Holding Back the Sauce', *The Guardian*, Saturday 22 May, available online at <http://www.guardian.co.uk/uk_news/story/0,3604,1222315,00.html> (accessed April 2007).

Orwell, G. (1998) *The Complete Works of George Orwell*, ed. P. Davison, 20 vols, London: Secker & Warburg; repr. 2002.

Shelden, M. (1991) *Orwell: The Authorised Biography*, London: Heinemann.

Swift, J. (1998) *Gulliver's Travels*, ed. P. Turner, Oxford: Oxford University Press.

Taylor, D. J. (2001) 'How Much Longer Can They Keep It Up?', *Guardian*, 27 August available online at <http://www.guardian.co.uk/g2/story/0,3604,542885,00.html> (accessed April 2007).

Chapter 6

How *Viz* made Britain ruder

Theo Tait

The end of the *Chatterley* ban in 1960; Kenneth Tynan's use of the word *fuck* on the TV in 1965; the Sex Pistols saying *shit, dirty fucker* and *fucking rotter* to a horrified Bill Grundy on *Thames Today* in 1976; the *Oxford English Dictionary*'s decision to admit swear-words in the mid-1970s – these are the familiar landmarks in the recent history of British public swearing. But the journey of *Viz* from obscure fanzine to mass-market 'arse-joke sales phenomenon' (in the words of one of its begetters) is surely as important as any of them. 'In England the gap between what can be said and what can be printed is rather exceptionally wide,' wrote George Orwell in 1941 (161). *Viz* emphatically filled that gap with endless references to farting, testicles, tits, bottoms, turds, piles, etc. The tabloids briefly manufactured a little outrage at the success of what they dubbed the 'four-letter comic'. But since then, *Viz* has continued to occupy a permanent and fairly uncontroversial position on shelves of the nation's newsagents.

Viz began in a teenager's bedroom in Newcastle. In 1979, a 19-year-old DHSS clerk called Chris Donald put together a rude 12-page comic with his younger brother Simon and a friend, Jim Brownlow. He gave it the apparently meaningless but somehow appropriate name *Viz*, printed 150 copies, and hawked it at a punk gig in a local pub. Priced 20p (30p to students), the comic sold out; and, slowly, with only two or three issues appearing every year, it built up a cult following. As its visionary founding editor sensed, *Viz* filled a hitherto unrecognized gap in the market. What the great British public really needed was a very sweary cross between the *Beano*, a fanzine, and a tabloid. Sustained initially by fanatical determination on the part of its editor, and the Tories' Enterprise Allowance Scheme, it was eventually picked up by an enterprising publisher in 1985. By the beginning of the 1990s, each issue was selling more than a million copies, making it the UK's fourth biggest selling magazine. *Viz*'s best-known characters – such as Roger Mellie the Man on the Telly, Buster Gonad and his Unfeasibly Large Testicles, Sid the Sexist, and The Fat Slags – became household names; the expression 'Fnarr! Fnarr!' entered the national consciousness.

'These were heady times for Britain's rudest magazine,' writes Professor

Humphrey Arseholes, Reader in Adult Comics and Jazzmags at Keeble College, Oxford, in his introduction to a selection of choice excerpts from the period, *The Porky Chopper*. 'The expletive hungry magazine buying public were snapping up rude words, like "beef curtains", faster than *Viz* could think them up. Along with milk men, Radio Three's *Test Match Special* and Broadmoor, *Viz* had become an institution' (Donald *et al.* 1993: 4). In its heyday it was read by 30 per cent of all British men between eighteen and forty, and admired by luminaries from Michael Palin to Keith Richards, Jilly Cooper to Alan Clark. Although sales declined as the 1990s progressed, it is still going strong today, with a quarter of a century of superior lavatory humour under its belt, and a still-solid, if much reduced circulation, of somewhere around 100,000.

Viz emerged in a recognizable shape over roughly five years and twelve issues, between 1979 and 1984. The first few issues contain the germs of its later format, but many of the strips are cruder, more anarchic, excessive, and violent, showing influences that would eventually be rejected, such as science fiction and American underground comics in the Robert Crumb tradition. Gradually, a tight formula emerged, which is still largely followed today: a mixture of cartoons, one-frame gags, take-offs of various tabloid and magazine features – exposés, readers' letters, photo-strip stories, adverts. During roughly the same time period, *Viz* built up its original core editorial staff, as Simon Thorp, a cartoonist from Yorkshire, and a 'lapsed botanist' named Graham Dury joined Chris and Simon Donald, with occasional but vital contributions from Jim Brownlow (Cook 2004: 40–3). Though the work of each individual cartoonist is identifiable, over time their disparate drawing styles became more similar, and a definite house style emerged.

Chris Donald explains in his memoir *Rude Kids* that there were two main types of *Viz* cartoon character. The first was what he called the Category A type: 'taking a recognizable stereotype and exaggerating it' (Donald 2004: 130). These included the famous Saturday night stereotypes, inspired by weekend visits to Newcastle's Bigg Market: The Fat Slags and Sid the Sexist, as well as other mostly self-explanatory archetypes, such as Spoilt Bastard, Mrs Brady – Old Lady, Student Grant, and Farmer Palmer ('Get orff moy laaa-aand'). These follow a rigid generic pattern: despite his chauvinist bravado, Sid is condemned to remain a virgin, and to be humiliated at the end of every strip, usually receiving a painful injury to his genitals. This kind of cartoon probably finds its ultimate expression in Simon Thorp's Eight Ace, the story of a thirsty family man. Each strip sees him sent to the shops with £1.49 by his wife to buy something important for the children (medicine, Sunny Delight, ready-meals). Unfortunately, £1.49 is the exact price of eight cans of cheap Ace lager. Each time he tells himself that he won't spend the money on drink – a resolve that he maintains right up until the moment that he arrives at the mini-market checkout. Each story ends with him vomiting and banging on his front door while the bairns go without: a parable of alcoholic backsliding, hard-edged but strangely affecting.

In each of these Category A cartoons, the formulaic nature is offset by the sharp draughtsmanship, the comic timing and the careful collection of social detail: Mrs Brady's perfectly rendered old lady-speak; the impassive face of the Sikh in the off-licence who serves Eight Ace; Sid's Geordie slang and his chat-up lines ('Hoo, Pet. My name's Sid. Do you like art? Well get a lurd of me cock, love. It's a masterpiece!" ') (*Viz*, 153, 2006).

Like most satirists, the authors of *Viz* seem to have been outsiders, slightly distanced from their social surroundings. The Donalds and Jim Brownlow lived in comfortable middle-class districts, but went to Heaton Comprehensive, a school that took tougher students from inner-city areas like Byker and Walker. 'Suddenly, for the first time you met all these hooligans,' says Simon Donald; his brother's biography details his dread of being picked off by bullies (Cook 2004: 12). There was also a class difference between their parents: their father was a milkman and oil salesman who scrimped and saved to buy a house in Jesmond, the district where their mother, an artist and a window dresser at Fenwick's, had grown up:

> Jesmond was a trendy, middle-class suburb, full of CND-supporting, Citroën-2CV-driving families, and Dad took great delight in poking fun and laughing at our 'lefty' neighbours. . . . Dad's parents were from Shieldfield, the neighbouring working-class suburb, and from what little I remember of them they had the same sense of humour. Nana Donald took to calling my uncle Jack 'Lord Shite' after he got himself a job as chauffeur for the Lord Mayor and started dressing in fancy suits.
>
> (Donald 2004: 6)

In all this, you can see the social geography of *Viz* sketched out in miniature. Many of their Category A characters come out of this social matrix, from violent, criminal working-class caricatures like Biffa Bacon and Rat Boy to the embarrassing middle-class characters – Student Grant and the beardy horrors later drawn by John Fardell, The Modern Parents and The Critics. Add in a some gently offensive regional stereotypes, such as Cockney Wanker and The Boy Scouse, a Liverpool scout troop dedicated to mugging grannies and twocking cars, and a few jabs at poncey let's-do-lunch Londoners (such as Dickie Beasley, the child advertising whiz) and you have *Viz*'s Britain. Occasionally, these sorts of strips also deal in topical satire: Baxter Basics, a Tory MP with revolting sexual habits, appeared briefly during the Major government's ill-advised public probity campaign.

What Donald calls the Category B type of cartoon was produced by 'parodying comic characters, rather than real people. These generally had a silly name and amusing appearance, no roots in real life, but were amusing none the less' (Donald 2004: 130). The classic examples are Buster Gonad and Johnny Fartpants (Figure 6.1), whose oversized testicles and violent flatulence, respectively, are always getting them into scrapes. Again, the formula is fairly rigid, a form of ironic tribute to the classic British post-war comic, particularly the *Beano* and the *Dandy*. A common scenario is that the character tries to solve problems for himself or other people using his unusual gift or possession. This usually backfires, often painfully, or reaches a slightly absurd happy ending. The comic scheme, like most comic schemes, is not very complicated: it lies in the contrast between the quaintly amusing and lovingly parodied comic book Britain – of vicars, local bobbies, teachers, bullies, roaming eccentric million-aires ready to hand out large amounts of cash, completely inconsequential punch-lines – and the grotesque or profane elements. Johnny Fartpants 'was going to be the ultimate *Viz* character,' explains Simon Donald, 'in that it was very much like a British comic and yet it was about schoolboy humour which had never yet been in print' (Cook 2004: 91).

Some of the best are the surreal variants, such as Gilbert Ratchet, drawn by Davey Jones, who started contributing to *Viz* in 1987. Gilbert is a young ama-teur handyman, who invents ludicrous solutions to bizarre problems. For example, he might meet a middle-aged man who will say something like: 'Damn it. I am keen sexual pervert, yet at present am unable to think of any bizarre and physically improbable activities whereby to procure carnal gratification' (*Viz*,

Figure 6.1 Johnny Fartpants.

44, 1990). Gilbert's inventions usually go spectacularly wrong, often dismembering a teacher or a vicar in the process. The strip usually ends in a very contrived misunderstanding, which leaves young Gilbert thwarted. 'I suppose he was inspired by Screwy Driver who used to be in the *Dandy*', Jones explains. 'Mind you, Screwy Driver tended to do less genital mutilation of vicars than Gilbert Ratchet' (Cook 2004: 115).

Various other types of comic strip have also been parodied: the long-running Billy the Fish is a tribute to Roy of the Rovers, while the Dandy's Black Bob, about a heroic border collie, was sarcastically reinvented as Black Bag, the Faithful Border Bin Liner. Similar in tone is Jack Black, a Blytonesque right-wing boy detective who spends his holidays getting sympathetic characters arrested for minor technical offences – closing down soup kitchens under obscure tax legislation, for example. He reads the *Daily Mail*, and in one episode has a slap-up tea with Hitler. Another long-running feature has been the photo-strips, parodying the photo love stories of *Jackie* and other girls' magazines.

But there is also a third prevalent type of *Viz* character, which falls somewhere in between Category A and B, and probably expresses the essence of *Viz* most economically. This is a character whose primary role is to be incongruously rude, by behaving badly in a way that ill befits his or her status, particularly by swearing. Characters in this vein include many *Viz* favourites: Paul Whicker, Tall Vicar, Roger Mellie the Man on the Telly, Postman Plod the Miserable Bastard, and Sweary Mary (Figure 6.2), right through to the very recent Friar Fuck, the Monk with Tourette's. The origin for this tradition is probably Jim Brownlow's single-frame Rude Kid jokes (see Figure 6.3), each featuring an exchange between a young child and his pleasant-looking mother:

> 'Come to the shops dear!'
>   'Fuck off!'
> 'What would you like for Christmas dear?'
>   'Fuck Christmas'
> 'Would you like a new pair of shoes dear?'
>   'Big Bollocks'
> 'Have you done your homework young man?'
>   'Knob cheese'

> (*Viz*, 1–12, 1979–84)

And so on. Rude Kid set a precedent: the success of these characters depends on the inappropriateness of their behaviour; and the quality, variety, and ingenuity of the obscenities they use. It's important, for instance, that Paul Whicker says 'Pick the bones out of that one, cunt bubble!' when he punches the man at the benefits office, rather than anything more prosaic (*Viz*, 10, 1983). Again, fairly intangible factors such as timing, precision, and allusion are very important. For instance, Roger Mellie's catchphrase is 'Hello, good evening and bollocks!' – a nicely turned version of David Frost's welcome.

Figure 6.2 Sweary Mary.

Figure 6.3 Rude Kid.

In many ways, the distinctions between these categories are blurred. Biffa Bacon, for instance, is both a Category A and a Category B cartoon, while all styles of *Viz* cartoon rely on similar techniques. Johnny Fartpants's single joke is sustained by the range of onomatopoeic noises accompanying each bout of flatulence: not just 'parp', 'rumble' and 'pump', but also 'quake', 'quack', 'oink', 'phoot', and 'phhrrapp!'; likewise Johnny's enthusiastic exclamations, such as 'Sew a button on this!' In the same vein is another Simon Thorp character, Finbarr Saunders and his Double Entendres, a variation on the third type of strip, in that his role is to perceive rudeness rather than act it out. Again, the simple premise is offset by the often very contorted innuendoes that he perceives everywhere ('This is quite a difficult tune to play – so we'll go slowly until you get your fingers round the hard parts'), and by his own baroque variations on the basic 'oo, er' of earlier, simpler times: 'fnarr! fnarr!', 'k-yuk! k-yuk!', 'yurk! yurk!' 'kwooo-ooooaaa-aaar!' And the Finbarr Saunders cartoons are as rigidly generic as Eight Ace, since they always end with him finally overhearing his mother and her genteel yet sinister boyfriend Mr Gimlet having sex – but mistaking it for something entirely innocent. (Mother: 'Ooh!

Mr Gimlet! What a fine tool you have!' Finbarr: 'Perhaps a hobby like fretwork would keep me out of mischief too!') (*Viz*, 28, 1988).

In his excellent short history of *Viz*, William Cook points out that at the time the only humour magazines available in 1979 were *Private Eye*, with its slightly smug political in-jokes, and the failing *Punch*. If you were too old for comics and too young for the *New Statesman* or the *Spectator*, you were left with the music magazines. Cook sums up the attraction of *Viz* very well:

> This was real schoolboy humour – the sort of jokes you heard behind every bike shed, from the roughest comprehensive to the poshest public school. You never laugh like you did at school, and reading *Viz* was like being back in the boys' bogs, sharing cigarettes and taking the piss out of the teachers. '*Viz* was into that humour that people only think they have with their mates,' says Andy [Inman, who ran the punk collective that *Viz* grew out of]. 'Lots of groups of mates have it all over the place, and if you could meet up with each other you'd probably have thousands of friends.'
>
> (Cook 2004: 23)

Features such as the letters page and Roger's Profanisaurus, 'an entertaining glossary of vulgarity, expletives, colourful obscenity and sexual euphemism' (front page, Donald, 1998), built partly from contributions by readers, made the magazine a sort of national forum for behind-the-bike-sheds-style chat.

At one level, the point of *Viz* was its rudeness: it was all about crossing lines that hadn't been crossed. '*Viz* had all this street language in it that had never been in print before,' Simon Donald points out. 'There were no magazines on the shelves at the time that had bad language in them apart from pornography' (Cook 2004: 23). No doubt its energy and its massive appeal came, to a large extent, from the unprecedented eruption of unofficial rude culture into a mass market magazine. In an era when traditional deference was breaking down, its icons of inappropriate behaviour, like Roger Mellie, Paul Whicker and Rude Kid, poked fun at middle-class institutions: the BBC, the Church, polite mother-hood. And it represented working-class experience in a form that was arguably more full-blooded, more engaged with the reality of life in Britain than much of the middle-class fiction of the time: 'If the future generations look back on the literature of the age,' remarked Auberon Waugh, 'they'll more usefully look back to *Viz* than they would, for instance, the novels of Peter Ackroyd and Julian Barnes, because *Viz* has got a genuine vitality of its own which comes from the society which it represents' (Cook 2004: 82).

There is a parallel, here, with punk – with which *Viz* shares a sweary, irrever-ent two-fingers-to-the-world attitude and a cut-and-paste style (the heading for the Letterbocks page, like many of Chris Donald's early designs, is clearly influenced by the famous cover for the Sex Pistols album *Never Mind the Bollocks*). Like punk, *Viz* was a dole-age rebellion against good manners, built out of junk culture. The *Viz* people have a fierce competence in low-brow culture – not only comics, but also tabloids, women's magazines, doctor jokes, porn, and useless celebrities – and their parodies are usually pitch-perfect. They are fluent in tabloidese, as this nonsensical exposé written by Chris Donald, entitled 'I made love to myself – why I watched', demonstrates:

> I'd had a few drinks and was feeling quite relaxed. Next thing I knew I felt my hand on my shoulder. Seconds later I was rolling around naked on the floor with myself. It seemed the most natural thing in the world.
>
> (*Viz*, 37, 1989)

Or this entry in the Profanisaurus:

> **charms** *n*. Of British tabloid journalism, the breasts. Usually prefixed 'ample'.
>
> (Donald 1998: 19)

Or the recent description of the invasion of Saddam's Iraq war as 'a war he was too cowardly even to start' (*Viz*, 126, 2004). Another instance of this is Top Tips, which started off as a brilliant parody of the dispiriting hints which used to be sent into housekeeping magazines:

> Cut along the edge of a tea bag and empty out the tea to make an ideal After Eight mint cosy. A. Asda, Castleford.
>
> (*Viz*, 50, 1991)

Yet, unlike punk, *Viz* is clearly not anarchic or furious – it's relatively gentle and precise, even slightly pedantic. Perhaps, as in most good satire, there's an edge of controlled rage in some of it – about the poverty of expectations, the sheer inanity of what was on offer in modern Britain. Striking examples of this include Chris Donald's brilliant sarcastic adverts: the immortal 'Raped? Burgled? Run Over? Why not call the Police?'; or the billboards glimpsed in the background of Billy the Fish, which read: 'Smoke Tabs . . . Eat Food . . . Drink Liquids . . . [partially obscured] it in your Bog' (Donald *et al*. 1993: back page). But clearly the parallel with punk only goes so far.

Indeed, it's clear that *Viz* is much more interested in being amusingly sweary than in actually being rude. Perceptions of offensiveness in language, of course, change with the times. In the nineteenth century, people worried about religious curses; in the mid and later twentieth century it was sexual swearing that exercised the moral guardians. Nowadays, the word *fuck* is thought to be only moderately offensive – it is not allowed on television before the 9pm watershed, but among consenting adults it has lost its power to shock. No one, according to the prevalent present-day sensibility, is really harmed by the reading of the word in private, of their own volition. Notions of decency and obscenity in themselves have lost much of their power: though some regard swearing with distaste, few see it as an offence against moral standards or God. Instead, words are more often perceived as rude if they cast offence in a particular direction: the obvious examples being the terms *nigger* and *Paki*, while *cunt* and *whore*, for instance, are regarded as unpleasant because they carry the implication of sexual humiliation towards women.

The humour in *Viz* mostly comes from the crossing of taboo lines that are increasingly perceived – certainly among its readership group – as being abstract, rather than to do with causing genuine offence. It has by and large avoided the genuinely and officially taboo areas of modern life. Racial stereotypes are mostly out of bounds: its most risqué moment was a one-off short cartoon in 1990 called The Thieving Gypsy Bastards, which was never repeated, after complaints from the race relations authorities. In a recent Gilbert Ratchet cartoon, Gilbert thinks about going down to the mosque to poke fun at the Muslims, but then decides that the local vicar is a better bet. By and large, explains Chris Donald, he 'forbade the use of the "C" word' out of distaste for it (Donald 2004: 156). The Fat Slags have been perceived, surely rightly, as being a sexist caricature; but the magazine as whole is quite carefully balanced: Sid the Sexist puts sexists themselves through the grinder.

Viz wasn't interested in being rude as part of a programme, unlike alternative comics of the period such as Ben Elton, who wanted to smash cultural and political taboos together. Rudeness, in *Viz*, is primarily a comic strategy – and actually a fairly delicate one. It relies on a fine balance of profanity and fastidiousness, even daintiness. As Jeremy Noel-Tod points out:

> The magazine's title sums up its trick of comic incongruity. 'Viz.' is one of the most pompously archaic monosyllables to which an English-speaker can resort (take, for example, the illustration of usage given by the Concise Oxford Dictionary: 'came to a firm conclusion, viz. that we were right'). Later, grosser imitations of the comic such as Zit and Spit missed the point: Viz may begin with a V-sign, but the joke is really on its own wrongness as a name for a rude comic.
>
> (Noel-Tod 2004)

To put the same point another way, a strip called 'Buster Gonad and his Fucking Big Bollocks' wouldn't have had quite the same appeal.

'I've heard many people say that Viz has only got one joke which it repeats endlessly,' says the *Guardian*'s political cartoonist Steve Bell.

> This is true, but only in the same sense that Poussin painted a lot of one-track, abstruse shepherd gags. For the begetters of Viz are true classicists of the toilet form. What is striking about their work is not its grossly explicit over-the-top rudeness but its classical restraint. . . . This is Neo-Classical Filth. For was not Rubens a Tit and Bum man?
>
> (Bell 1989)

This is hyperbole, but it analyses well how *Viz* works – the series of ironic contrasts on which it is built: between constraint and complete lack of it; between economy of means and subject-matter, and its wild variety of filth; innocence and naughtiness; basic, babyish humour and recondite cultural references. Probably the clearest example of this is the Profanisaurus. Here are some fairly typical examples from the 1998 version, which highlight another favourite *Viz* trick – the clash of registers between official and unofficial language, between high and popular culture:

> **anus** *n*. Doctor-speak for the *council gritter* (*qv*).
>
> **lucky Pierre** *n*. In *botting* circles, the busiest botting link in a three-man *bum chain* (*qv*); the filling in a shirt-lifter sandwich.
>
> **step on a duck** *v*. To create a quack; fart. *orig*. From a remark made by King Edward VI upon hearing a hunting companion sound his *trouser trumpet* (*qv*). 'Sir, I may be mistaken, but I do believe you have stepped on a duck'.
>
> > (Donald 1998: 5, 51, 79–80)

Chris Donald makes it clear that restraint was an important part of his comic technique: 'I find wanking a tasteless subject for humour (unless, for some reason, monkeys are involved)' (Donald 2004: 147). Wanking jokes have usually taken a highly recherché form in *Viz*: he's referring here to Mickey's Monkey Spunk Moped, about a lad who relies on simian semen to run his bike; another example is Captain Oats, 'the polar explorer who loves to explore his *own* pole', but is constantly thwarted in his attempts to do so.

In his classic article on saucy seaside postcards, 'The Art of Donald McGill', Orwell writes that 'the outstanding, all-important feature' of McGill's postcards is their obscenity. 'It is by this that everyone remembers them, and it is also central to their purpose' (Orwell 1941: 159). The mere suggestion of sex, when the subject was strictly patrolled by censorship laws and official morality, was enough to make them funny, to provide the hinge for a joke. In *Viz*, by contrast, they were free to depict any bodily functions they felt like, but the editors soon realized that there was limited comic mileage in simply depicting tasteless subjects. And over time, Simon Donald's cruder cartoons were complemented by Davey Jones's more recondite and demented ones, making the contrast between comic strip form and content ever more pronounced and bizarre: Arse Farm, The Vibrating Bum-Faced Goats, and so on.

Even so, *Viz*'s massive sales growth in the first years that it was sold nationally, and its declining circulation thereafter, are probably explained by the initial thrill of seeing taboos smashed; and the diminishing returns thereafter. The often-heard complaint that it's 'not as funny as it used to be' – apparently first made by Mark E. Smith of The Fall back in 1986 – no doubt has the same explanation. The first-ever sight of a cartoon about a farting boy is hard to reproduce – even though the magazine by and large got funnier and sharper during the first 20 years of production. This dynamic perhaps also accounts for some of the comic's failures: its repetitiveness, the fact that its cartoons sometimes seem bored of their own infantile limitations – seem only to be enacting their own pointlessness.

Viz is both traditional and very modern. The Fat Slags, for instance, is a more explicit continuation in the vein of the saucy postcard or the *Carry On* film – 'something as traditional as Greek tragedy,' according to Orwell (1941: 156). It follows the age-old conventions of 'low' comedy, and tells of unchanging human types, bawdy goings-on and involuntary bodily motions. This is the Carnivalesque, with its grotesque bodies, and unruly crowds – poking fun at noble intentions and authority, giving expression to what Orwell calls 'the Sancho Panza view of life' (162):

> He is your unofficial self, the voice of the belly protesting against the soul. His tastes lie towards safety, soft beds, no work, pots of beer and women with 'voluptuous' figures. He it is who punctures your fine attitudes and urges you to look after Number One, to be unfaithful to your wife, to bilk your debts, and so on and so forth.
>
> (163)

But another equally important strand in *Viz* is a distinctively modern or post-modern one: ironic, parodic and culturally competent, completely submerged in throwaway culture (for example, see Figure 6.4). And it's this characteristic combination of bawdiness and savvy irony which has been most influential on British culture at large. Famously, the tone was taken up by the Lads' Mags, initially in the form of *Loaded* 1994 (which ran an interview with Chris Donald in its first issue). To take one representative example: *Viz* ran a series of amusing advertising campaigns featuring ridiculous 1960s pornographic photographs. One showed a woman wearing a fur coat and hat, warming her bottom in front of a period gas fire. The caption read: '*Viz* – the magazine this woman's arse is talking about'. There was a speech bubble coming from her bottom, which read: 'Have you seen the latest *Viz*? Very funny. Made *me* laugh anyway' (Donald 2004: 333–4). Clearly, this advert was not titillating: it was funny because it caricatured porn. Yet exactly the same style – the ironic captions, the same behind-the-bike-shed atmosphere – has been used by Lads' Mags to sell what are definitely soft porn magazines, bringing an all-important sense of humour and camaraderie to the essentially lonely business of having one off the wrist. Irony has helped to make the Lad, roguish and unabashed about his sexuality, socially acceptable. The magazines and their style have spread like a virus to America, where Ariel Levy describes their success just after the turn of the century:

> a porny new genre called the Lad Mag, which included titles like *Maxim*, *FHM*, and *Stuff*, was hitting the stands and becoming a huge success by

Figure 6.4 Viz anthology front cover in the style of a Lad Mag cover.

delivering what *Playboy* had only occasionally managed to capture: greased celebrities in little scraps of fabric humping the floor.

(Levy 2005: 2)

Without wishing to blame *Viz* for the pornification of the Western world, I suppose one could conclude that taboo lines are there for a reason. If you cross them – even, like *Viz*, with fairly innocent intent – then things change, often in quite profound ways. But that's another story.

References

Bell, S. (1989) 'Dandy Filth', *Guardian*, 27 November.

Cook, W. (2004) *25 Years of 'Viz'*, London: Boxtree.

Donald, C. (2004) *Rude Kids: The Unfeasible Story of 'Viz'*, London: HarperCollins.

—— (1998) *Roger's Profanisaurus*, London: Routledge.

Donald, C. *et al.* (1993) *The Porky Chopper: Selections from 'Viz' Issues 48 to 52*, London: John Brown.

Levy, A. (2005) *Female Chauvinist Pigs: Women and the Rise of Raunch Culture*, New York: Free Press.

Noel-Tod, J. (2004) 'Tarquin Hoylet, he has to go to the toilet', *Sunday Telegraph*, 8 October 2004 available online at <http://www.telegraph.co.uk/arts/main.jhtml ?xml=/arts/2004/10/10/bodon10.xml> (accessed April 2007).

Orwell, G. (1941) 'The Art of Donald McGill', in S. Orwell and I. Angus (eds) *The Collected Essays, Journalism and Letters of George Orwell*, vol. 2: *My Country Right or Left, 1940–1943*, Boston: Nonpareil Books, 2000, pp. 155–65.

Viz (1979–) issues 1 through 153 (1985–7 London: Virgin; 1987–2001 London: John Brown; 2001–3 London: IFG; 2003– London: Dennis).

Chapter 7

Bosom of the nation

Page Three in the 1970s and 1980s

Rebecca Loncraine

> The *Sun* did not invent the bosom, any more than it invented the permissive society.
>
> (Lamb 1989: 110)

The *Sun* has been the best-selling daily paper in Britain since 1978. Its topless pin-up page, known as Page Three, first appeared in the early 1970s and it soon became the paper's mascot. Like the busty wooden carvings perched on the prow of seventeenth-century galleons, the Page Three girl is the figurehead for the *Sun*, symbolizing its irreverence, its no-nonsense explicitness and, some would say, its misogyny. Page Three has its origins in the 1960s' permissive society; it emerged from and continued to participate in wider debates about the nature of obscenity, about what it was acceptable to show in public, and, in turn, how to define what was in fact 'public'.

Page Three was first mentioned in parliament in the early 1970s during a debate on the Bill to ban nudity from public hoardings during which MPs discussed whether or not a newspaper was a public display. By printing photographs of topless women the *Sun* provoked questions about the nature of the print media and freedom of the press, but most of all it tested the limits of what was offensive. In an article in the women's pages of the *Sun* in December 1969, Deirdre MacSharry declared that 'the year 1969 was when men and women took their clothes off in public in a startling manner. Now ... we have got over the shock and nudes are no longer regarded as rude'. But not everyone had got over the shock. As we shall see, the journalists and editors at the *Sun* carefully shaped its Page Three to skirt the boundaries of rudeness, test the limits of public tolerance and to generate free publicity.

The politics of Page Three have been as shifting as those of the *Sun* itself (which changed from supporting Labour in the 1960s and early 1970s to Conservative in the late 1970s and 1980s). The ways in which Page Three changed during these years reflect wider shifts in British cultural and political life. But Page Three not only mirrored wider shifts in values, it also shaped them, becoming part of the public culture it exploited in order to make the *Sun* the most profitable product in Murdoch's media empire.

Public nudity was fashionable in Britain in the late 1960s. Naturism, a movement which had begun in the utopian socialist movements of the nineteenth century, became popular among a wider public. In France women began to sunbathe topless on beaches, and even in chillier Britain, coastal councils were forced to consider ending the laws prohibiting topless sunbathing. But this was more than a swimwear fashion: Marilyn Yalom writes, somewhat wryly, that for some women the 'desire to attain a new measure of equality with men and to exercise autonomy over their bodies began with the removal of the tops of their bathing suits' (1998: 180). Baring all had become a statement of protest against older generations and more traditional values. But it wasn't just on the beach that the new fashion for public nudity was exposed. The 1968 Theatre Act abolished the Lord Chamberlain's right to censor the theatre; numerous theatres expressed their new freedom by featuring nudity on stage. In 1969 the West End showcased several productions that included nudity, such as *Hair* and *Oh! Calcutta!* If, in reality, it was only a small number of hippies, naturists, actors and sunbathers who were taking their clothes off in public, the worlds of fashion, advertising and the media made it seem as though public nudity was ubiquitous. This was an attempt to appear counter-cultural, but it was also an attempt to boost sales: the mild shock created by these pictures of naked people grabbed consumers' attention.

Public nudity had become so fashionable by the early 1970s that it provoked a defensive outburst from the naturist movement itself. In the December 1970 issue of *Health and Efficiency* magazine, the naturist monthly, Alex Watford wrote an outspoken editorial. 'Where exactly do we stand in this permissive age,' he asked, 'surrounded throughout the land by flaunting of the nude and near-nude human form on posters, in films, magazines, and on theatre stages?' '*We* were the hardy pioneers,' he complained, 'who took all our clothes off long before the mere idea of a body in the buff could be projected with as much freedom and vigour as we find today at pop festivals, in papers and magazines, on screens and stages. But the permissives of 1970 are not even grateful!'

It was the broadsheets, surprisingly, and not the tabloids that first printed nudes in their advertising. For instance, in July 1969, the *Sunday Times Magazine* included a fashion feature showing a double-page full frontal shot of a woman from the waist up, wearing only a necklace. The caption read: 'It appears that people can't wait to take their clothes off these days. The growing fad for nudity is everywhere.' An advert for a weight-loss machine called 'The Automasseur' appeared in the *Times* in October 1970. The advert showed a naked woman pictured from behind, turning to the side to reveal her breasts. 'How to be a Good Loser' was the headline. In contrast, the *Daily Mirror*, the bestselling daily paper in Britain, did not feature adverts or fashion pieces which used images of nudity.

Rupert Murdoch bought the ailing *Sun* from IPC in 1968 and re-launched it in 1969. He already owned the *News of the World* and wanted a daily as well as a Sunday newspaper. He decided he would re-launch on the back of what had been dubbed the 'permissive society'. The front page of the first edition in November 1969 was a mission statement. The *Sun* was 'opposed to Capital Punishment, apartheid, racism and the Vietnam war, and in favour of the permissive society'. 'From day one,' write Peter Chippindale and Chris Horrie, 'the *Sun* had chosen sex as the battleground for the coming circulation war with its rivals' (1992: 23). The *Sun*'s main competitor was the bestselling *Mirror*. But Larry Lamb, the paper's first editor, and Murdoch had noticed that the *Mirror* had failed to engage fully with the social changes brought about in the late 1960s (excepting the sterling efforts of Marje Proops, the *Mirror*'s agony aunt).

British popular newspapers have always included pin-ups, but the *Sun* exploited the 1960s fashion for public nudity and merged it with an older tradition of popular newspaper pin-ups – pictures of 'pretty girls' – pioneered by the *Daily Mirror* in the 1940s. 'The *Sun* is always best for nudes' was the tagline. The paper covered stories about the fashion for baring all, accompanied by photographs, with no hint, of course, of pubic hair (the print unions would later register their discontent by drawing a pubic hair on to a Page Three photograph, thus forcing the paper to withdraw that edition). A naked woman appeared in the very first issue. A nude groupie was featured with her back to the camera in a photograph with the Rolling Stones. In its second edition, the *Sun* dared to go a little further and revealed a woman's nipple. Uschi Obermeier, a model who had joined a hippie commune in Berlin, was pictured topless, wearing jeans. By telling stories of nudity in public, the *Sun* had a legitimate excuse to publish pictures of naked and scantily clad people without appearing exploitative or strictly taking responsibility for them. But Murdoch recognized regional differences in attitudes to nudity, and in the early 1970s a man was employed for the Irish editions to draw clothes on to any photographs which showed bare bottoms or breasts.

The first real 'Page Three' appeared in November 1970, on the *Sun*'s first birthday. The front page of the birthday edition announced, 'The *Sun*, your newspaper, is one year old today. It is Britain's brightest, most irreverent, most unpredictable newspaper.' The paper announced a 'birthday suit girl, p. 3'. Stephanie Rhan was pictured naked and in profile, sitting in a meadow. This picture was in the style of photographs in *Health and Efficiency* magazine, and it differed very little from pictures of naked bodies printed in news stories about public nudity. What was new about the photograph was that the *Sun* had *staged* it specifically for their page three.

Stephanie's nude debut did not, however, instantly usher in the institution of the Page Three girl. Like many British institutions, Page Three did not appear overnight. It would take a further four years for topless photographs to become synonymous with the *Sun*. Lamb explains that 'The evolution of the Page Three girl was a gradual process' (1989: 111).

The next nude on page three appeared in March 1971, and she proved hugely important in the development of 'Page Three'. 'The Lovely Lady who Shocked the Top People' was the headline of a story about a full-page photograph of a naked female model that had appeared the day before in a broadsheet. Ignorant of the *Times*'s history of printing pictures of naked women, readers inundated the gentlemanly paper with letters of complaint. 'It has long been apparent that advertisers have lost all sense of scruple,' wrote T. Abbott from Martyrs Green in Surrey, 'and for a quality paper such as yours to support this is very saddening' (*Times*, March 1971). The *Sun* reproduced the image on page three. 'Top people,' they wrote, 'don't go for bottoms' (March 1971). This suggested that *Sun* readers would not be shocked by the picture. The *Sun* was taking a risk, testing its readership, challenging them to be shocked like the 'top people' (read as 'toffs'). As far as we know, the *Sun* received no complaints. Lamb admitted that the *Times*'s audacity in publishing this photograph inspired him to push topless pin-ups further in the *Sun*.

A month after the *Times* nude, a photograph of a naked Helen Mirren, starring in a new Ken Russell film, was printed on page three; Mirren has recently played Queen Elizabeth II in the film *The Queen*. 'They're off! It's the Big Nude Show!' described the 1972 Miss Nude USA beauty contest (June 1972). Once readers were accustomed to seeing stories about public nudity accompanied by revealing photographs, the *Sun* could drop the news stories altogether and just print their own staged nudes as straightforward pin-ups. But it was not until the mid-1970s that the term 'Page Three' was coined.

The *Sun* was becoming increasingly confident about printing photographs of topless women (though not of white British women, as I will explain) but they were still anxious not to alienate more old-fashioned readers. The *Sun* aimed to appeal to youthful adults, but also wanted to steal the *Mirror*'s older, more traditional, readership. Appealing to both groups meant walking a political tightrope between youthful liberalism and more traditional values. This was achieved through the juxtaposition of different types of articles in the layout of the page. Anxious articles about shifting values appeared adjacent to photographs of topless women. Next to Angela was an article with the headline 'Stop the Moral Rot, Says Archbishop' (April 1971). 'New Clean-up Plan' for 'the peddlers who flaunt sex in public places' declared another story placed next to a photograph of a woman in a bikini. The report went on to ask 'Does Smutty Britain Offend You?' (August 1972)

Beyond stories expressing moral uncertainty, the paper went further, using page three as the place to display what some saw as the other, darker side of the new permissiveness. Anti-permissives thought the shifting moral sands would bring about the collapse of the social order, the explosion of the nuclear family, and unleash dangerous sexual and violent appetites. James Callaghan, on replacing reformer Roy Jenkins as home secretary in 1967, had said he would 'call a halt to the advancing tide of so-called permissiveness'.

The *Sun* made sure they appealed to this perspective as well as to the pro-permissive point of view. These different attitudes clashed with one another on page three to create a heady cocktail that simultaneously celebrated liberalization and expressed shock and anxiety about the (perceived) impact of this liberalization.

Tales of family breakdown and domestic and sexual violence filled page three in the early 1970s. The paper was full of old-fashioned court reporting. The criminal and family courts could, from the conservative point of view, be seen as dealing with the social collapse brought about by moral pluralism and social liberalism. In the early 1970s, in a disturbing strategy, stories of violence towards women, including rape, appeared on page three almost daily. Alongside Sue Shifrin in bikini bottoms was the headline 'Young Juliet Forgives the Romeo who stabbed her' (February 1972). The report told how a man had attacked his girlfriend with a knife. Next to a photograph of a topless model was a report on the case of actor Darren Nesbitt, accused of beating his wife, Anne Aubrey. The article provided gruesome details of the attack: 'He grabbed her breast, bruising it badly', said the report (March 1973). Next to topless Pru in huge bold type was the headline 'Girl, 14, Tells of Rape by Angels in Cave' (May 1972). The article gave the horrific details of a girl's ordeal at the hands of a group of Hell's Angels. The headline 'Country Doctor Raped Me After Tips on Yoga' appeared next to smiling Marilyn, from Portsmouth, who, the caption explained, was 'the first model to appear as a full frontal nude in the centre pages of *Playboy* magazine' (March 1973). This juxtaposition of explicit articles about sexual violence with photographs of topless women appealed to the prurient moral hypocrite. But it was also a way of appealing to older, more traditional readers, whose moral outrage at the pictures of nudity was acknowledged and accommodated by the accompanying tales of social collapse.

The *Sun* has always told tales of both sex and violence. Billy Bragg commented on this in his 1984 song 'It Says Here'. The tabloids, sings Billy, 'offer you a feature/On stockings and suspenders/Next to a call for stiffer penalties for sex offenders'. But in the late 1970s, when Page Three had become an established feature of the *Sun*, the paper moved reports of violence against women, and rape cases in particular, out of page three and on to other pages. Lamb admits, dishonestly, that 'Occasionally, when by accident a story of rape or other male violence towards women appeared on the same page [as topless models], there were those who suggested that such a juxtaposition was not a good idea – and they were usually right' (1989: 117). It was not that photographs of topless women were considered offensive or rude in themselves, but by the late 1970s the particularly nasty prurient titillation created by placing articles about sexual and domestic violence in juxtaposition to such images was considered to be inappropriate and offensive. It is no coincidence that by the late 1970s second-wave feminism had begun to make an impact on mainstream British media and culture.

Naked men and exotic foreigners: Page Three in the 1970s

The stereotype of the Page Three girl is the white British busty *Carry On*-style Barbara Windsor bubbly blonde, like the bosomy cartoon characters of the seaside postcard. But when the *Sun* first started to make page three the page for nudes, both women *and* men appeared with their clothes off. The history of the *Sun's* relationship with its women readers makes sense of this. When the *Sun* was first launched by IPC in 1964 under Hugh Cudlipp, the paper actively courted a young female readership. The paper was produced with the help of extensive new market research that told Cudlipp that there was a youthful, educated and semi-affluent lower-middle-class couple who were not catered for by the newspapers. On the front page of Cudlipp's debut *Sun* in 1964, the paper wrote its manifesto: it would be 'a new newspaper, born of the age we live in'. Under a series of headings, including 'The New Woman', the paper declared:

> The present role of British women is the most significant and fruitful change in our social life. Women are no longer trapped between four walls. They are released from household drudgery by labour-saving devices, gadgets and intelligent home planning. In 1938 only one married woman in ten went out to work: the figure is now one in three and will soon increase. The emancipation of their minds has been accelerated at a fascinating pace by wider human contact outside the home. Women are the pacesetters now.

The women's pages were called the Pacesetters. They took the frank coverage of issues such as contraception, marriage, divorce and sex, pioneered by Marjorie Proops in the *Mirror*, and pushed them further to produce outspoken liberal articles that Lamb described as 'feminine feminism'. These pages set a precedent that would develop in the 1970s into *Cosmopolitan* magazine. Some of the journalists who worked on the Pacesetters pages would move to *Cosmopolitan* to become the magazine's founding journalists. Lamb thought it was important to retain the unique Pacesetters pages. In his memoirs he says: 'The Murdoch *Sun* was the first newspaper clearly to recognise the obvious truth that every other reader is a woman. Not only that, we were in tune with the new mood of *feminine* feminism. . . . From Day One we addressed ourselves to women in a direct and, I hope, non-patronising fashion' (Lamb 1989: 56).

The fashion for public nudity was unisex and this was reflected in the *Sun* in its early years. Women's breasts were the racy, daring body parts the *Sun* needed to display to ensure its status as risqué; in terms of men's bodies it was their exposed buttocks that stretched the limits of public decency. In December 1969, for instance, a man's bare bottom was emblazoned across the front page. The picture had been taken at a Rolling Stones concert. 'The Stones' music was too hot for this fan. He took his clothes off and left' was the caption beneath a photograph of a naked man climbing over a stunned crowd. In the early 1970s photographs of naked or scantily clad men often appeared alongside topless or naked women. These photographs were always to accompany a 'news' story about public nudity (a fashion show, a film, a play, a rock concert). This was a unique moment in the history of Page Three, when women readers were acknowledged and addressed in every part of the paper. Pictures of naked men disappeared from page three in the mid-1970s as the paper's confidence in its new topless female pin-ups grew and as its commitment to make the whole paper appealing to women faded. With the shift from covering tales of public nudity to creating staged topless pin-ups, images of naked men were dropped.

In the 1980s another attempt to address women readers with a male pin-up resurfaced with the short-lived 'Page Seven fella'. While the shots of women in the 1980s were more erotic and explicit than they had been in the 1970s, the images of men in the 1980s were more conservative than they had been in the days of unisex nudity. Men's buttocks were rarely revealed; this was perhaps due to Kelvin MacKenzie's worry that the Page Seven fella might make the paper popular with gay men. It was the naked male body that was too risqué to expose in the tabloids.

In Britain, we think of Page Three as a national institution, but in the early 1970s white British women rarely appeared topless on page three; British models wore skimpy outfits or turned to one side to hide their breasts. Page Three developed as the paper's mascot by featuring photographs of topless northern European and French women. At this time British politicians were arguing about the pros and cons of joining the European Economic Community (Britain finally joined in 1973); heated debates about the relationship between the different nations of Europe were taking place throughout the early 1970s. In a semi-serious lecture given in 1972, Robert Megarry declared:

> Whereas in England all is permitted that is not expressly prohibited, it has been said that in Germany all is prohibited unless expressly permitted and in France all is permitted that is expressly prohibited. In the European Common Market no-one knows what is permitted.
>
> (Ratcliffe 2003: 133)

The relationship between different European cultures was, in a way, being explored on the *Sun*'s Page Three in the early 1970s. These relationships, however, did not concern trade tariffs and import duties, but the topic of public nudity. Page three showed northern and continental Europeans as far more liberal in this issue than the coy Brits.

The *Sun* began featuring topless women by drawing on the stereotypes of sexually liberal northern Europeans and French women sunbathing topless on the French Riviera. The paper pictured numerous northern Europeans, like Lia, a 'Swiss Miss', German Uschi Obermeier and Swedish Ulla Lindstrom. Stephanie Rhan, the notorious 'birthday suit girl', was from Munich. 'I Say, Waiter! There's a Bare Bosom in My Soup' was the headline of one article in 1971. A woman was pictured standing in the sea up to her waist. Holiday-makers had been complaining about the 'craze' for toplessness among the 'gay young things' of the Riviera. The paper even made an explicit connection between the EEC and Page Three in a boxed caption next to topless Valerie: 'Britain's all-out Common Market Bid Brings Bosom Friends like Topless Valerie', said the caption (August 1971). Topless modelling was presented as foreign and leisured, but accessible to the British reader via newly affordable package holidays, advertised very often in the *Sun*. The subtext was that if Britain joined the EEC, the values of the permissive French would creep over the Channel.

The *Sun* also featured numerous photographs of black women on page three in the early 1970s. The very first photograph of a front-facing topless woman to appear on page three (not the coy side-on images like that of Stephanie Rhan) was of a black model, Venetia Day. The photograph was taken at the Olympia Motorcar Show in London. Venetia was pictured lying prostrate across the bonnet of a racing car. She was presented as exotic, like the expensive racing car she was draped over. Minerva Smith was presented in more overtly racist terms. She was described as 'a real exotic fruit, in fact, with a taste for bananas'. The caption went on to say: 'She comes from Guyana, where her favourite delicacy grows on trees. But she grew tired of frittering life away in the sun and decided to split for a fruitful career in Britain' (March 1972). 'Mynah Bird' was described as 'Nigerian-born', which suggested she could have immigrated to Britain (May 1972). Controversies over immigration and race relations were at a peak in the early 1970s. Overblown fears about 'tides' of immigration from Commonwealth countries had whipped up racist prejudice, as expressed by the formation of the National Front in 1967 and Enoch Powell's inflammatory 'Rivers of Blood' speech in 1968. Both Labour and Conservative governments of the late 1960s and early 1970s responded to these anxieties and prejudices in the same way with a raft of Anti-immigration Acts to placate the right (1962, 1968, 1971), and a series of Race Relations Acts to placate the left (1965, 1968, 1976). By featuring black models who were African-born British immigrants, the *Sun* was purposely touching on a controversial topic.

In 1972 the *Sun* made a movement in the opposite direction, taking an anti-racist stance. 'Harmony Week' showcased the need for racial equality. 'We're Winning the Race War' was the front page headline on day one of Harmony Week (July 1972). The report went on to explain that research 'gives heartening evidence of the way white and coloured families are getting on with each other'. Articles on 'Why Enoch is Wrong', and the lives of African-American actors Sidney Poitier and Fred Williamson, followed. A week of black pin-ups was part of Harmony Week. Beneath the headline 'Black is Certainly Beautiful', a model called Josy leapt in the air. The caption explained: 'she is from Guadeloupe in the French West Indies'. The following day Minerva Smith appeared again and the caption said: 'The shape of race relations gets a real uplift from Guyana-born model Minerva Smith' (July 1972).

To the twenty-first-century reader the racism at work in these photographs is a form of contemporary offence that goes beyond even the sexism. But in the early 1970s the *Sun* designed the pin-up page through exploiting conflicting ideas about race, titillating readers by yoking together new ideas of polite respect for black immigrants with an older colonial racism. These black models were presented in terms of a variety of racial stereotypes. For one, they were viewed essentially in terms of their skin colour. The paper was perhaps also drawing on a colonial racism which regarded the publication in the media of photographs of topless black women as acceptable. The tradition of displaying such pictures went back as far as the 1920s, in photographs in *National Geographic*. But 'Harmony Week' gave these photographs a veneer of contemporary progressive politics. As did the *Sun*'s claim that they were 'opposed to . . . apartheid . . . and racism'. The *Sun* fought for its position as the newcomer on Fleet Street through flirting with boundaries of what was acceptable and what would cause offence by carefully exploiting racial and national stereotypes; the point was not simply to show topless women: it was about who was exposed (foreigners and black immigrants) and, implicitly, who was not (white British women).

'Get tough on these filth sellers'

The purpose of Page Three was not only to titillate loyal *Sun* readers. The *Sun*'s mascot was designed to provoke a response from various groups outside its target readership. The *Sun* likes nothing more than to publicize criticisms of its topless photographs. Lamb admits that Page Three became important 'mainly because they got us talked about' (1989: 111). The 1970s witnessed not only the emergence of Page Three but also the birth of the Page Three critic. Lamb explains that 'the more the critics jumped up and down, the 'more popular the feature became' (1989: 115). The paper soon realized it could gain free publicity by provoking attacks from people outside its target readership. Clearly it would not be in their interests to offend loyal readers (as it would do later in its misguided coverage of the Hillsborough disaster) but offending middle-class moralists, bureaucrats, toffs and prudes appealed to the *Sun*.

One of the first times the *Sun* grasped the opportunity for publicity provided by its critics was in the case of the 'Silly Burghers of Sowery Bridge'. In 1970 a council in Yorkshire banned the *Sun* from Sowery Bridge public library because, they said, it contained too much sex. The *Sun* was outraged. 'We should have been thrown out of better places than this,' said an article on the incident (February 1970). In 1972 the *Sun* printed stories about *Pornography: The Longford Report*, which was published that year. Lord Longford had headed an investigation into pornography in the UK. He was convinced that 'pornography does indeed represent a problem' (Longford 1972: 12). The committee set up in 1971 to investigate pornography was made up of a cross-section of society, including bishops, housewives, students and aristocrats, and even Kingsley Amis, Cliff Richard and Jimmy Savile (those well-known experts on sexuality). The report directly criticized the *Sun*, describing its success as based upon 'sex and punchy radicalism' (323). 'It is generally recognised in Fleet Street,' wrote the report, 'that the *Sun's* formula has had a depressing effect on other popular rivals' (322). A few days later the *Sun* featured a photograph of Karen Boyes in a bikini alongside the headline 'Get Tough on these Filth Sellers says Lord Porn'. Two days later the *Sun* showed an upside down photograph of a model in a bikini. The caption said: 'Why Maggie is upside down', and the article went on to say: 'Longford's opinion is that the *Sun* is thriving on an "Antipodean blend of erotica" . . . Maggie is upside down because we wanted to give you a chance of seeing things the way Lord Porn does' (September 1972). Paradoxically, the *Longford Report* had concluded that the *Sun* was more conservative than the broadsheets in its use of language, particularly of swear words and descriptions of body parts: 'the "quality" papers,' said the report, 'were often prepared to provide more explicit detail in covering sex cases, and also to make use of less acceptable language' (Longford 1972: 323). The *Sun* had no interest in printing the less critical appraisals of the paper in the *Longford Report*; they were only interested in publicizing the criticisms.

In 1973 Alexander Lyon, a Labour MP (Clare Short's husband), complained about the *Sun* in the House of Commons during a debate on the Indecent Displays Bill (which Short referred to 13 years later during the debate on her Bill to ban Page Three). The *Sun* leapt at this opportunity. Next to a photograph of topless Linda Munro was the headline 'What Three MPs say about the Lovely Ladies in the *Sun*'. The paper explained that 'the *Sun's* gorgeous girls came under attack from three Labour MPs in the Commons yesterday' (April 1973). Lyon said that a person sitting next to someone reading the *Sun* on a train might well take offence.

Vocal disapproval of the *Sun* by establishment figures helped the paper build and promote its image as being outside the Establishment. The more criticism the paper received for its pictures of naked and semi-clothed women (and men), the more determined it became to push them to the forefront of its emerging brand identity.

Rise of the mummy-babies: Page Three in the 1980s

The *Sun's* circulation figures overtook those of the *Mirror* in 1978, and Murdoch's paper became the best-selling daily in Britain. By this time the topless pin-up page was firmly established as 'Page Three'. A year later, Margaret Thatcher and the Conservatives were brought to power. Thatcher talked in vague terms about what she termed 'Victorian values', citing free-market economics, self-reliance, morality, charity and private property. Nobody seems to have been able to pin her down on what she and her fellow Conservatives meant exactly by 'Victorian values', but what this rhetoric did signify was a move away from the post-war values of social liberalism, the welfare state, moral pluralism and secularization. This rhetoric was picked up by the media and 'Victorian values' became a catchphrase for Thatcherism.

Page Three gradually altered in the 1980s in accordance with this shift away from the values of the permissive society; also reflecting the conversion of Rupert Murdoch and Kelvin MacKenzie, the *Sun*'s bold, brash new editor, who took over from Lamb in 1981, to Thatcherism. MacKenzie used the rhetoric of a return to Victorian values as an excuse for a proliferation of scandalous stories about sex, including the outing of gay men. Cate Haste, writing on sexuality and politics in the 1980s, explains that 'exhortations to restore conservative mores gave the press license to deal in sexual "scandal" in the guise of moralizing on transgressions' (2002: 300).

The style of Page Three changed. The naturist-style nudes of the 1970s, shot outdoors in lush meadows with little make-up and no props were no longer in tune with the times. Page Three became more eroticized, with shoots taking place indoors. Models were heavily made up, wore lacy lingerie, and had gimmicks and props. Linda Lusardi, for instance, appeared wearing a jockey's hat, wielding a whip. Another model wore a mortar board and held a long wooden ruler in her hand. Models got much younger. Sam Fox, the most famous Page Three girl of the 1980s (who recently shocked the *Sun* by coming out, transforming herself from heterosexual sex symbol into gay icon) made her debut in the *Sun* just after her 16th birthday (she was 15 in the original photograph sent to the paper). The style of Page Three in the 1980s was more akin to soft-pornography, with models being called 'Page Three Pets', like the 'Penthouse Pets'. This more soft-porn style chimed with the agenda of a return to Victorian values by presenting nudity as erotic and naughty, rather than zesty, healthy, naturist and liberated, as it had been presented in the 1970s.

By the 1980s public nudity was no longer fashionable. In mainstream British culture it was as though everyone had put their clothes back on except the Page Three girls. Page Three began to stand out and receive attention, most famously from MP Clare Short. In January 1986 a Bill was brought before parliament by Conservative MP Winston Churchill to extend the Obscene Publications Act to broadcasting. This Bill was partially inspired by Christian conservative campaigner Mary Whitehouse, who found in the Tories a sympathy she had not until then received from politicians. Clare Short, Labour MP for Birmingham Ladywood, was present during the debate on the Bill and she suggested that the definition of obscenity as anything which 'was likely to deprave or corrupt' was hopelessly inadequate. Short suggested amending the definition of obscenity to include a reference to anything which demeaned women and sex. 'The definition of deprave and corrupt is a bad one,' she said, 'we need to move in another direction. We must move against material that degrades women and human sexuality' (*Hansard* 1986: 626). Short was worried that the Tory's measure would make sex education material illegal. She was trying to replace the definition of obscenity born out of a Christian moral framework with one which looked more to a post-1960s second-wave feminist agenda. She opposed Churchill's Bill because, in her view, it did nothing to stop demeaning images of women being broadcast. Whilst arguing against this Bill she remarked that she would bring in her own, which would focus on the problem as far as she saw it. What became an attempt to introduce a Private Member's Bill to ban Page Three emerged out of a wider debate, in a post-*Chatterley* trial world, about the nature and definition of obscenity, about what was offensive in public.

In her statement to the House of Commons in March 1986, introducing her Private Member's Bill, Short explained that she was offering 'A Bill To make illegal the display of pictures of naked or partially naked women in sexually provocative poses in newspapers' (Short 1991: xiii). Her Bill would only apply to newspapers. She wanted to apply the Indecent Displays (Control) Act, which prevented nudity from appearing on public hoardings, to newspapers, raising the question of whether or not a newspaper was a public display. The Bill was passed by a majority of 41. Robert Adley opposed the Bill, and rightly pointed out some of the most obvious problems with it: 'who will decide', he said, 'whether a woman is or is not partially naked, and whether her pose is or is not sexually provocative' (Short 1991: xvii). He went on to say, 'There are a few pleasures left to us today. One that I enjoy is sitting in an underground train watching the faces of the people who are pretending not to be looking at Page 3' (Short 1991: xvii). Adley felt unable to admit whether or not he enjoyed looking at pictures of topless women, and was forced to take a contorted route in defending the *Sun*, saying he enjoyed looking at people who were pretending not to look at pin-ups. These rhetorical gymnastics reveal an underlying anxiety about an MP admitting to looking at Page Three.

In her account of the debate, Short describes how she encountered rudeness of a different sort: 'As I spoke . . . a large clump of Tory MPs began to giggle and chortle and make crude remarks about me, my Bill and my body' (Short 1991: 4). *Hansard* provides no descriptions of the body language, noises and mutterings of MPs during debates. In this case it simply says: '[*Interruption*] . . . [*Interruption*] . . . [*Interruption*]' (Short 1991: xxiv). At this time the House of Commons was not recorded on camera. By giving an account only of what MPs say during speeches, and not the more physical and audible elements of debating, *Hansard* omits the more impolite aspects of the House, and creates a very partial picture of parliamentary debates. The controversy in the media over this Bill focused as much on the treatment of Short by other MPs as it did in the topic of Page Three. After the radio news played a recording of the debate many people wrote to Short to express their outrage. One 'life long Conservative' woman wrote: 'I was absolutely disgusted at the way you were treated' (Short 1991: 30). Another said: 'I was furious to hear the guffaws and sexist remarks from some of your fellow MPs when I listened to Parliament on the radio. . . . As a woman, and knowing that there are only 25 women MPs in Parliament, I feel totally alienated by that institution' (Short 1991: 32). These critics took offence at the treatment of Short by fellow MPs, whose attacks on her seemed to go beyond the customary ya-booing, to become both gendered and unusually personal. There was a woman at the helm, but Thatcher was noticeably silent on Short's Bill. No doubt she was anxious not to damage her relationship with Murdoch.

Other women who wrote to Short pointed out an inconsistency in attitudes to women's breasts, comparing Page Three pin-ups with the debate about women's right to breastfeed in public. 'The matter was highlighted for me,' wrote one woman, 'because I had just returned from the doctor's with my baby. The person sitting next to me was reading *The Sun*, and these girls were openly displayed, yet it occurred to me that if I were to start breastfeeding my baby, there would be more than a few raised eyebrows' (Short 1991: 120). In another letter a woman complained that 'Page 3 displays seem to be perfectly acceptable yet breastfeeding mothers are not . . . in one large department store, my friend and I were asked to stop as it "wasn't very nice for the other customers"' (Short 1991: 121). Breastfeeding in public became an issue of comparison with Page Three in part because of the style of the Page Three girls in the 1980s. One journalist said that the Page Three girl was characterized by the 'unusual combination of nursing mother on top and schoolgirl below' (Taylor 1991: 33). In an article in *Cosmopolitan* magazine in June 1986, Sally Vickers noticed the same thing:

> The standard Page Three whopper girl is invariably baby-faced and smiling with all the ingenuous expectancy of a child . . . while sporting a pair of breasts that look as though they belong to a lactating mother. Why is our national prototypical sex object a sort of mummy-baby?

It was the inconsistency in attitudes towards the exposure of women's breasts in public, based on some idea of the purpose of that exposure (breast-feeding versus titillation, air-brushed image versus the real thing) that these critics objected to. In the *Sun*'s attack on Short that followed her Bill, the paper described her as 'sour'.

The body style of the Page Three girls of the 1980s was at odds with the wider fashionable image of women as tall, angular Material Girls in Armani suits with shoulder pads. Yalom suggests that the post-war 1950s 'big-busted' pin-ups 'carried a clear message for women: your role is to provide the breast, not the bread' (1998: 138). This 1950s busty ideal was an expression of anxiety about women's entry en masse into the economy during the war, and an exhortation to them to return to the domestic sphere. Despite the rhetoric of a return to Victorian values in the 1980s, there was a woman Prime Minister, and the independent, professional woman was both a highly fashionable image and becoming a reality. The *Sun*'s 'mummy-babies' were, perhaps, as well as being a reinvention of the bawdy blonde of the seaside postcard, an expression of anxiety about women's increasing public authority and status, and a conservative nostalgia for the idea that women's primary role was domestic and maternal.

In the tradition of showcasing Page Three critics established in the 1970s, the *Sun*'s response to Short's Bill was to publicize it proudly. Short admitted that MPs 'rarely have time to take [Private Members' Bills] further. But it can be a good way of raising new issues' (Short 1991: 3). There was never any real danger that she would succeed in banning Page Three. The *Sun*, however, presented Short as a genuine threat. The story dominated Page Three through-out March 1986. Headlines read: 'Michelle Fights for Page Three' and 'Fighting the Battle to Save Page Three'. The *Sun* announced that 'a massive save Page Three campaign was launched yesterday to block killjoy MP Clare Short'. The paper presented Short as a prude, and printed a cartoon of her clothing a statue of naked Eros with a pair of trousers, shown in Figure 7.1. 'She objected to Eros

Figure 7.1 *Sun* cartoon.

showing his bum', was the caption. The truth was that the *Sun* had stopped printing photographs of men's naked buttocks in the mid-1970s, deeming them too risqué and offensive, too rude for their male readers. 'The battle's really on to Save Page Three from prudes' declared the paper. The *Sun* also accused Short of being a hypocrite for not supporting Churchill's Bill to extend the Obscene Publications Act. The paper did not distinguish between the different positions occupied by Churchill and Short: between a traditional Christian position concerned with keeping nudity and sex out of the public sphere, and an attempt to carve out a separate feminist definition of obscenity. The *Sun* presented these two distinct grounds for establishing a definition of offence as identical and indistinguishable.

In the 1970s and 1980s, Page Three confronted readers with their assumptions about what a newspaper was and about the meaning of the freedom of the press. Page Three pictures were designed to provoke readers to make a judgement about what was rude in public. It skirted the boundaries of public tolerance, titillating working-class (male) readers ('the folks', as MacKenzie called them) by brushing up against the values of what was presented as polite, stuffy, society. The pin-ups were also purposely designed to annoy people outside the paper's target readership (traditionalists, prudes, middle-class women). Turning from a front-page headline about the troubles in Northern Ireland, the miner's strike or the Falklands conflict, the reader was faced with a picture of a smiling topless woman, a picture that positioned the reader somewhere on the delicate boundary occupied by the *Sun* between entertainment and discomfort.

Bibliography

Barcan, R. (2004) *Nudity: A Cultural History*, Oxford: Berg.

Chippindale, P., and Horrie, C. (1992) *Stick It Up Your Punter! The Rise and Fall of the 'Sun'*, London: Mandarin.

Hansard (1986) *The Parliamentary Debates*, Sixth Series, Volume 96, Session 1985–6, pp. 624–9, London, Her Majesty's Stationery Office.

Haste, C. (2002) *Rules of Desire: Sex in Britain: World War I to the Present*, London: Vintage.

Lamb, L. (1989) *Sunrise: The Remarkable Rise and Rise of the Best-Selling Soaraway 'Sun'*, London: Papermac.

Longford (1972) *Pornography: The Longford Report*, Sevenoaks: Coronet.

McNair, B. (2002) *Striptease Culture: Sex, Media and the Democratisation of Desire*, London: Routledge.

Ratcliffe, S. (ed.) (2003), *Oxford Dictionary of Quotations by Subject*, Oxford: Oxford University Press.

Sandbrook, D. (2006) *White Heat: A History of Britain in the Swinging Sixties*, London: Little, Brown.

Short, C. (1991) *Dear Clare: This Is What Women Feel about Page 3*, ed. K. Tunks and D. Hutchinson, London: Hutchinson Radius.

The *Sun*, 1964–2006.

Taylor, S. J. (1991) *Shock! Horror! The Tabloids in Action*, London: Bantam Press.

Yalom, M. (1998) *A History of the Breast*, London: Pandora.

Part III

The limits of rudeness

When Saturday comes
The boundaries of football rudeness

Tony Crowley

It is clear that the conventions which govern the use of 'rude' language in public discourse have altered over a generation. It is possible to imagine a Tory patriarch like Ted Heath or a Labour leader like Harold Wilson referring to members of their governing cabinet as 'bastards' in private conversation. But it is difficult to imagine either of these British Prime Ministers using this description in public. Perhaps more importantly, it is open to doubt whether the use of such a term, even if it slipped out by mistake, would have been reported by the leading newspapers and media outlets of the day. It is more likely that the desire on the part of the gatekeepers of culture to protect the linguistic propriety of the political field would have outweighed the temptation to print a controversial story.[1] Yet John Major's position as Prime Minister in 1993 appeared wholly unaffected by his leaked admission that he didn't sack rebel ministers after a parliamentary vote of confidence because he didn't want 'three more of the bastards' conspiring against him. Indeed the comment may well have enhanced Major's weak image in the eyes of the electorate. His successor, Tony Blair, at least in the early days of his premiership, actively cultivated an association with the 'bad-mouthed' boys and girls of Cool Britannia and his Press Secretary and confidante Alastair Campbell gained a reputation for his use of expletives in his dealings with the media.[2] There seems then to have been a modification to the 'structure of feeling' associated with this aspect of rudeness in British society. But there is one place in Britain which has been almost automatically linked with forms of rudeness which are socially unacceptable; a location where offensiveness, crudity, insulting behaviour and nastiness constitute not so much the exception as the norm. Or at least this is how it appears in the social imaginary. The aim of this chapter will be to explore this arena in order to determine what it reveals about both British society and its boundaries of rudeness. The site to be considered is the Premiership football ground, when Saturday comes.[3]

One text which focuses much of the debate both about rules of public rudeness and football fans is Tony Harrison's *V.*, first published in 1985 in the aftermath of the Miners' Strike against the Thatcher government. It is perhaps difficult to recall some twenty years later the furore which this poem, or at least a film of the poet reading it, caused in British public life. First scheduled to be broadcast on Channel 4 in a mid-evening slot, the film was re-scheduled for 11.30pm on 4 November 1985 in response to the furious protests of self-appointed moral guardians, the Tory press, and Thatcherite politicians. The *Daily Express* inaccurately described the poem as a tribute to the Miners' leader Arthur Scargill (the epigram is a quote from Scargill on his father's belief in the power of words), and warned that a 'torrent of foul language will be seen in a Channel 4 programme by respected Newcastle poet Tony Harrison' (Harrison 1989: 42). And the *Daily Mail* described the film as containing 'a torrent of four-letter filth . . . which will unleash the most explicitly sexual language yet beamed into the nation's living rooms' (Harrison 1989: 40). Both papers quoted Tory MPs. Gerald Howarth asserted that 'this is another case of the broad-casters trying to assault the public by pushing against the barriers of what is acceptable' and described Harrison as 'another probable Bolshie poet seeking to impose his frustrations on the rest of us' (Harrison 1989: 41). While Teddy Taylor 'appealed to Channel 4 chiefs to see sense' and observed that 'obviously Channel 4 is the place for experiment, and for a bit of variety, but a poem stuffed full of obscenities is clearly so objectionable that it will lead to the Government being forced to take action it would prefer not to have to take' (Harrison 1989: 41). The action which the government was allegedly reluctant to undertake was the setting up of a new media monitoring unit; the fact that the Home Secretary had already announced the creation of the Broadcasting Standards Council was conveniently forgotten.

The Tory reaction to the poem was constituted by two ideological tendencies. The first was the concern for the damaging effect of 'bad language' on the moral fabric of British social life. The articulation of this worry by a party which treated established communities – not least mining villages – with con-tempt, which bred cynicism with its corruption of public office, and which promoted laissez-faire deregulation by its neo-liberal privatization mania, is noteworthy. The second ideological factor was the Thatcherite hatred of the working class, manifested not least in its attitude towards football fans. Yet despite the fact that what Harrison had produced in his poem was precisely the image of the football supporter which most Tories held (an uneducated, drunk and violent working-class man), it was the 'foul language' fear which dominated the response, an indication in itself of the special place which 'bad language' has in the Tory code of values.

One of the aims of *V.* is to speak for those who are politically and culturally silenced, to articulate the sentiments of the socially inarticulate. And it does so in a nuanced, powerful and seductive manner in a crucial section in which the football fan, writing graffiti on the headstones in a graveyard, makes an accusation against the poetic persona:

> *Don't talk to me of fucking representing*
> *the class yer were born into any more.*

Yer going to get 'urt and start resenting
it's not poetry we need in this class war.
(Harrison 1989: 22)

The poet responds by challenging him to authorize his graffiti by inscribing his name:

He took the can, contemptuous, unhurried
and cleared the nozzle and prepared to sign
the UNITED sprayed where mam and dad were buried.
He aerosolled his name. And it was mine.
(Harrison 1989: 22)

What Harrison attempts is a partial identification between the poet and the working-class football fan; the suggestion is that this is perhaps what Harrison himself would have been without the scholarship to a grammar school and the university education in Classics. The rude anti-social football thug is made to represent, patronisingly at times, the person lacking the benefit of culture and education; in its extreme form, the untamed 'foul-mouthed' racist.

V. is by no means Harrison's best work, but it is a bold and challenging piece which uses vernacular experimentation in the service of a critique of the divisiveness, bitterness and social violence caused by Thatcherism. And while its presentation of particular forms of unity as the means of resolving social division is in fact exclusive (heterosexual domesticity is the model), the poem articulates a keen sense of the historical and material basis of the aesthetic, as its ending demonstrates:

Beneath your feet's a poet, then a pit.
Poetry supporter, if you're here to find
how poems can grow from (beat you to it!) SHIT
find the beef, the beer, the bread, then look behind.
(Harrison 1989: 33)

Yet although *V.* presents an angry denunciation of Thatcherite ideology and its effects, as noted earlier it also colludes with that ideology in its representation of the football fan as the site of anti-social behaviour, the product of a failure of education and culture, in short the embodiment of rudeness. It is with the behaviour of that stereotypical figure that the rest of this essay is concerned.

Bourdieu's model of social practice offers a means to analyse, at the level of language, the injustices of class in contemporary Western societies. Those at the bottom of the social order are dispossessed and disadvantaged by the division of linguistic and cultural capital which is structurally tied to the distribution of economic capital. The poor are effectively socially silenced by their use of illegitimate language, often in the form of awkwardness, incoherence or unacceptable 'rudeness', when confronted by contexts which demand specific forms of legitimate language. Thus in *V.* the football fan is sensitive to the social implications of the linguistic differences between his own speech and that of the poet. Responding to the poetic persona's use of the word 'aspiration' the skin retorts:

> *Aspirations, cunt! Folk on t'fucking dole*
> *'ave got about as much scope to aspire*
> *above the shit they're dumped in, cunt, as coal*
> *aspires to be chucked on t'fucking fire.*
>
> (Harrison 1989: 17)

The skin responds angrily to the use of the Latinate 'aspiration' and his violent rejection of the poet's patronizing effort to treat him as though he were actually silent and thus to speak on his behalf is prompted by a pun on the name 'Rimbaud' (which he hears as 'Rambo'). In answer to the attempt to include him in the poem – 'the reason why I want this in a book/'s to give ungrateful cunts like you a hearing!' – the skin replies:

> *Ah've told yer, no more Greek. . . . That's yer last warning!*
> *Ah'll boot yer fucking balls to Kingdom Come.*
> *They'll find yer cold on t'grave tomorrer morning.*
> *So don't speak Greek. Don't treat me like I'm dumb.*
>
> (Harrison 1989: 19)

V. is in part a poetic exploration of linguistic capital and its social power. The poetic persona in this account has the practical sense and social competence which derives from a particular educational and cultural training. His language conforms to the structural demands of a specific discursive field and is therefore recognized as legitimate; he is empowered to speak. And since 'all linguistic practices are measured against the legitimate practices, i.e. the practices of those who are dominant' (Bourdieu 1992: 53), the skin, lacking such competence, is doomed to speak a language which is classified as illegitimate, one which falls outside the boundaries of acceptable speech and which is thus unheard or misrecognized. A scene from another literary text illustrates Bourdieu's point. In Irvine Welsh's *Trainspotting* two characters are facing theft charges in court. One, Renton, is able to manipulate the code of legitimate language to present his defence. Asked by a magistrate if he stole books to sell for drug money he answers:

> – Naw. Eh, no, your honour. They were for reading.

Renton's self-correction (naw–no) represents a move towards conformity with the rules of formal discourse demanded by the context of the law court. The shift is consolidated in his response to the magistrate's scepticism about the likelihood of his reading Kierkegaard:

> – I'm interested in his concepts of subjectivity and truth, and particularly his ideas concerning choice; the notion that genuine choice is made out of doubt and uncertainty, and without recourse to the experience or advice of others.

Renton's co-accused, Spud, replies to the magistrate's question about stealing to pay for heroin:

> – That's spot on man . . . eh . . . ye goat it, likesay.

Sentenced to ten months in prison (Renton receives a fine and a suspended sentence), Spud can only mumble:

> – Thanks . . . eh, ah mean . . . nae hassle, likesay . . .
>
> (Welsh 1993: 165–6)[4]

This representation of the language of the working class echoes that made by an early twentieth-century British sociologist, C. F. G. Masterman, in his *From the Abyss: Of Its Inhabitants: By One of Them* (1902). Writing as a member of the working class, like Harrison, Masterman represents its speech as a form of silence, noting for example that working-class speakers 'never reach the level of ordered articulate utterance; never attain a language that the world beyond can hear' (Masterman 1902: 20). Yet Masterman's work offers another account of a crowd of working-class men:

> They drifted through the streets hoarsely cheering, breaking into fatuous irritating laughter, singing quaint militant melodies. . . . As the darkness drew on they relapsed more and more into bizarre and barbaric revelry. Where they whispered now they shouted; where they had pushed apologetically, now they shoved and collisioned and charged. They blew trumpets, hit each other with bladders; they tickled passers-by with feathers; they embraced ladies in the streets, laughing generally and boisterously. Later the drink got into them, and they reeled and struck and swore, walking and leaping and blaspheming God.
>
> (Masterman 1902: 3)

Rather than silence or awkward articulation, Masterman describes an excess of noise: cheering, laughter, singing, revelry, shouting, trumpets, swearing and blaspheming God. But Masterman's account ultimately supports Bourdieu's theoretical distinction between legitimate and illegitimate language: it is not that the working class, or indeed other marginalized groups, do not speak, but that their words do not belong to what Masterman calls 'ordered articulate utterance'. The working class is not silent, it is socially silenced by symbolic power; its speech becomes mere noise, inarticulacy, or rudeness.

Masterman's carnivalesque representation of the working-class crowd at the turn of the century sounds remarkably like a scene from contemporary football before a big game or after an important win. Yet an account of the behaviour of football crowds as simply chaotic and carnivalesque is as misleading as one which depicts such crowds as composed of the socially offensive thugs of the Thatcherite social imaginary. Both versions depict the football crowd as essentially random, disorderly and threatening, and thus not able to be understood by measured analysis. However, my point in this essay will be that the activity of the football crowd – the singing, the shouting, the movement, the laughter – is open to explanation by means of an application of Bourdieu's account of the legitimacy of specific modes of behaviour in a particular context. With regard to language, many of the speech acts of football fans are unacceptable beyond the walls of the stadium; within the ground they are subject to the rules and norms of a social field which constitutes legitimate and illegitimate speech. When Saturday comes the boundaries of rudeness change.

Before attempting an analysis of the conventions and the functions of football rudeness it is worth making two related points. First, the norms are historically specific: things which were acceptable in the 1970s are clearly no longer tolerated. Examples at Premiership grounds include chants which openly threaten violence ('You're gonna get your fucking heads kicked in', 'You're going home in a fucking ambulance') and racist songs, noises and chants (this will be considered later). Second, the composition of the football audience has changed for a number of reasons: the modifications to the stadiums after Hillsborough, the trendiness of football after Italia 1990, the glamourization of the game through satellite television coverage, corporatization and the consequent massive increases in ticket prices, to name but a few. Football is no longer simply a working-class game – at least in terms of those who go and watch it regularly. But despite the fact that the conventions and the nature of the audience have been transformed, behaviour in the stadium is still manifested in patterns which, though flexible, are analytically comprehensible. There are things which are acceptable and things which are, to use a key phrase, 'not on'.[5] For example it isn't on to sing another club's song, except perhaps in a mocking manner. It would be peculiar to sing on your own for any length of time (though shouting a comment is acceptable). It would be extraordinary to praise an opposition player lying injured; though it would be unusual not to applaud any seriously injured player as he left the ground. Interrupting a minute's silence in memory of the dead is unacceptable and if it occurs is usually attributable to a few individuals; organized chanting over the silence would represent a serious departure.[6] It is permissible to laugh if the referee runs into a player of the opposing team, but not if two of your own players collide . . . and so on. More than anything else, it is possible, if not expected, to be rude, either about the opposition, or, more infrequently, about members of your own team. But the sense of what is rude in this context is socially distinct. The rudeness of Harrison's skin or Spud in *Trainspotting* is the result of the process whereby working-class people are denied access to forms of linguistic capital and are thus produced as ignorant (in the neutral sense of the term). The rudeness of the football ground is different: rather than unknowing, the rudeness of the football fan is a form of deliberate and circumscribed offensiveness.[7]

If someone were to shout an insult at a stranger or group of strangers in the street or in a park they would be liable either to a response from that person, or, in given circumstances, an intervention by the forces of the State. Yet the following are all commonplaces inside football grounds: 'You're shit and you know you are', 'Who the fucking hell are you?', 'fuck off X' . . . Why would this be offensive in one instance and taken as normal or standard in another? The answer lies precisely in the fact that these are *generic* chants shouted or sung by thousands of people in a specific context. Rather than insults in the familiar sense, these are formulaic expressions in which the particular content is overridden by the nature of the act to which they belong. When a crowd chants 'the referee's a wanker', what is not in question is the private behaviour of a given individual (it's unusual for a referee's name to be used). Instead an illocutionary act is performed whose force is that of a general expression of antagonism. But in order for a performative to occur there have to be conventions which govern its use and form. For example, such a chant would rarely occur before the match started and never when the referee has just given your own side a penalty. Moreover only minor alterations can sensibly be made to the form: 'the linesman is a wanker' would be peculiar ('fuck off linesman' is the accepted call); 'the referee's a bastard', or 'the referee's a Scouser/Geordie/Cockney' are permissible, though 'the referee's an idiot' and 'the referee's a bigot' would be unlikely if not impossible.[8] Likewise with the other examples given above: 'you're no good and you know you are' wouldn't do, nor would 'you're rubbish'; 'Who the bloody hell are you?' would sound peculiar, as would 'bugger off X', 'go home X' and so on. The point about this type of performative is that it needs to be as conventionally offensive as possible. Yet even if these aren't insults in the ordinary sense of the term, they still seem to be expressions of extreme forms of rudeness; but if that were their function then they would have to be taken as clear failures. Given that one of the purposes of intentional rudeness is to inflict harm upon another, then the chanting of football songs at players or the referee seems to be peculiarly ineffective. This seems to be well recognized, not least in the testimony of ex-players that the taunts of a crowd actually spurred them on, or in the fact that referees make unpopular decisions constantly and seem little swayed by the words directed against them. Moreover few football fans seem to think that their words have much effect in this sense. But then the question arises: Why, given their practical inefficiency as insults, are such chants sung? The answer lies not in the antagonistic illocutionary force but in the perlocutionary effects of the rude chanting: the function of these songs is not to insult, but to produce a communal bond and identity through repeated performances of empty hostility.

The apparently excessive rudeness at football grounds constitutes the ongoing performance of a particular type of identity which demands specific forms of knowledge (if, what, when, how things can be articulated). This identity is not so much concerned with loyalty to the club or even the team (though both are of course included) since the reality is that both club (in terms of ownership) and team (in terms of personnel) can change radically whilst still attracting support. Being a football fan, rather than simply being a supporter of a club, is a question of occupying a specific social space and time and performing communal acts of identity. One such act is the chanting of (and listening to) songs whose exaggerated rudeness exemplifies the intensity of the identification. Football fans sing and shout in ways which are shared and which are socially unusual (the same chants anywhere else would infringe the law). The chanting of what sounds like abuse, but which is more like the production of commonality, is one of the elements of being a fan (and the fans of particular clubs share the, often traditional, rude songs and chants of that club). In this sense the boundaries of rudeness belong precisely to the constitutive boundaries of identity.

There are songs and chants which, if still rude by normal standards, include forms of irony, mockery or wit. Beating a team easily sparks the chant 'Can we play you every week?', or, hitting two targets at once, 'Are you X in disguise?' – where X is the name of a local rival, thus suggesting that both teams are poor. Players perceived to be overweight are doomed to hear 'Who ate all the pies? Who ate all the pies? You fat bastard, you fat bastard, you ate all the pies'. The arrival of a small number of visiting fans is often met with 'What's it like to see a crowd?' One player, Andy Goram of Rangers, was diagnosed with a form of schizophrenia and was greeted by: 'Two Andy Gorams, there's only two Andy Gorams'. The shout when Liverpool scored against Swiss team FC Basle was 'You're not yodelling any more'. Parody is a familiar technique, as in opposing fans' version of the Liverpool song 'You'll Never Walk Alone' with the chorus 'You'll never work again', referring to the high unemployment rates in the city during the 1980s and 1990s. The folksong 'In My Liverpool Home' (not in fact sung by Liverpool supporters) is recast as 'In your Liverpool slums, in your Liverpool slums, you look in the dustbins for something to eat, you find a dead rat and you think it's a treat . . .'; and in the same vein Manchester United fans sing 'Feed the Scousers, do they know it's Christmas time?', to the tune of Live Aid's 'Feed the World'. Wittier chants are often responses to insults from opposing fans. When Everton supporters mocked Swindon followers with the threat of relegation, 'going down, going down, going down', they were met with the rejoinder 'so are we, so are we, so are we . . .' And when Liverpool reached the Champions League final in 2005, held in Istanbul, their fans' answer to the condescending 'Champions League? You're having a laugh' was 'Champions League? We're having Kebabs'. In response to the taunt 'you're not famous any more', made by Chelsea fans at Liverpool's ground, the home fans took to chanting 'history, history, you can't buy history', and singing 'Money Can't Buy You Love'. Another reference to the dubious wealth of the Chelsea owner Roman Abramovich was made by the fans of Norwich, whose managing director happens to be a celebrity chef: 'We've got a supercook, you've got a Russian crook'.

There are, however, songs and types of chanting which are rude and socially offensive in other ways. Communal expression of sexism is relatively rare at football grounds, though given the dominant culture of male heterosexuality, sexist sentiment is never far away. The song aimed at David Beckham which referred to his wife ('Posh Spice takes it up the arse') is a good example of this form of chanting, which tends to be personal and specific rather than generic.[9] The same is true of the more recent development of homophobic abuse. One player, Graeme Le Saux, was constantly baited with references to homosexuality and anal sex; suspicion focused on the fact that he didn't read the tabloids and had cultural interests which differed from those of most footballers. And opposing fans frequently taunt the fans of Brighton FC (Brighton was for a long time Britain's gay capital) with 'we can see you holding hands'. But there is one mode of rude chanting which is hardly heard at the grounds of Premiership football clubs, and this is surprising given its prevalence in the previous generation. What strikes anyone who attended first division football matches in the 1970s and 1980s in Britain about today's Premiership games is the almost complete disappearance of racist abuse. Harrison's *V.* serves as a reminder that it wasn't always so:

> Jobless though they are how can these kids,
> even though their team's lost one more game,
> believe that the 'Pakis', 'Niggers', even 'Yids'
> sprayed on the tombstones here should bear the blame?
> (Harrison 1989: 16)

It should be made clear that what is not being argued is that racism has disappeared from football, nor that those who attend the games are not racist, nor that it is changes in the audience that have led to the silencing of racist abuse (middle-class racism runs quite as deep as its working-class counterpart). Nonetheless, it is a fact that racist chanting is very rarely heard at Premiership grounds and it is worth pondering the causes and implications of this change in the boundaries of permissible social rudeness on Saturday afternoons. Among the many reasons two particular and one more general suggest themselves. The first has to be the sheer number of black players in the game and their achievements. The fact that for a considerable period black players have been among the outstanding players in the Premiership makes the expression of a particular type of racism awkward (it's hard to call someone lazy or talentless for example if they have just scored a brilliant goal for or against your team). On its own, however, it is doubtful whether this would have been enough, as was demonstrated by the treatment meted out to John Barnes when he played for the English national team in the 1980s. A second factor which changed the attitude to black players in football was the set of anti-racist strategies introduced by the major football organizations, including the clubs, in the 1990s (principally the 'Kick Racism Out Of Football' campaign). This includes, in the Premiership grounds, regular anti-racist announcements before games, in signs at the ground and in the programme, and the making of racist chanting an offence liable to expulsion. It is also questionable, however, whether this would have worked (how can large numbers of people be ejected for singing a racist song?) without a third factor. This was the slow but evident change in the structure of feeling associated with race and racism in British society in the past generation.[10] Again this is not to underestimate the depth to which racism runs in contemporary Britain, but it is to recognize an important social shift in process. There are complex reasons for this development, demographic, economic and cultural, but among other factors State intervention has been important: explicit ordinances have included a mix of education, with the introduction of clear anti-racist policies in schools and the active promotion of multiculturalism, and law, with the Race Relations Act (1976) and its amendments (2000 and 2003 – the latter to conform to European Union policy). Whatever the precise causes, the net effect of the shift is evinced by the fact that not only is racist abuse rarely heard in Premiership grounds, but that when black England players were racially abused in a game against the Spanish national team in Madrid in November 2004 the outcry was based on the sense that 'we don't do that sort of thing'.[11]

Such a sentiment is clearly predicated on the cultural hegemony of anti-racism in the game. And one of the implications of the role of the State in the forging of this development may be to give those opposed to State intervention on such matters pause for thought; for all of the attacks on Political Correctness this is one area where it has been successful. Of course, as was stated earlier, this is not to claim that football is free from racism since this would be ludicrous; cultural hegemony does not permeate social reality. There are very few Asian players, almost no non-white managers or administrators, and for a sport dominated by black talent there are few enough black faces in the crowds. But to those who would challenge the extent of the success of anti-racism in football, it is worth pointing out that Premiership football grounds are one place in Britain where it is unlikely that a fit and talented non-white man will be racially abused or that children will hear racist comments; and in both cases if the offence takes place there is immediate recourse. A generation ago racist rudeness was part of the social competence of the football fan. These days you can be rude at Premiership football grounds, but the boundaries of rudeness have altered such that the socially offensive practice of racism is disallowed. The rules, the game and the field have changed.

Notes

1 Pierre Bourdieu uses the notion of a social 'field' as a structured set of contexts in which individuals act; distinct fields demand the use of various forms of capital (economic, cultural, symbolic, linguistic) and permit the conversion of one form of capital into another (Bourdieu 1992: 57–65, 229–51).

2 The shift is not confined to Britain. In 1992 the Irish Taoiseach (Prime Minister) Albert Reynolds described a point made to him by a journalist as 'crap'; it caused a furore and despite his citing a dictionary definition to defend his use of the word to mean 'nonsense' he was forced to withdraw and apologise. Ten years later the leader of the Irish Seanad (Senate), Mary O'Rourke, dismissed a political opponent with the same term without reaction. In the USA in July 2005 Henry Kissinger regretted the comment made in 1971, revealed in declassified state documents, that 'the Indians are bastards' (President Nixon, his interlocutor, called the Indian Prime Minister Indira Ghandi an 'old witch'). Evidently having a different sense of the limits of linguistic rudeness, Vice-President Cheney was overheard on television in June 2004 telling one of his political opponents to 'go fuck yourself'. In October 2004 George Bush, on the campaign trail, called a reporter 'a major league asshole'. In an electoral year their words seemed to do little serious harm.

3 Because of the demands imposed by Sky television, many Premiership games no longer take place on Saturday afternoon, but that remains the residual focal point for British soccer fans. I am drawing on my own experience as a life-long Liverpool fan and a regular at Anfield. This means of course that the evidence is partial, in the sense of limited, but the point is to make a general case and not one specific to Liverpool or Anfield. I refer in the essay to Premiership games only; the claims made here *do not* apply to non-Premiership games.

4 Both Harrison and Welsh represent a working-class speaker who has managed to acquire legitimate language by means of his education. The socially mobile members of disadvantaged groups are of course usually the most linguistically adept in being able to use a variety of codes.

5 'Not on' is originally a sporting usage: 'Acceptable; played according to the rules of a game (originally esp. in *Snooker*); conforming to a standard of behaviour, etc.; practicable, feasible. Freq. in negative contexts, esp. in *it's (just) not on*' (OED). Its first recorded instance is from 1935.

6 Taunting references to the death of officials and supporters of Manchester United at Munich (1958), or Liverpool supporters at Hillsborough (1989), are met with vitriolic abuse and sometimes violence. The bitterness of the rivalry between these two clubs led, in a recent example, to Liverpool fans chanting gleefully about an injury to a United player. The fact that the crowd's reaction turned when it became clear that the injury was serious, and the fact that there was an apologetic response later, proves the rule.

7 The semantic history of 'rude' records this distinction. The OED gives the senses: 'Lacking experience or skill *in*, without proper knowledge *of*, unaccustomed *to*, something', first used in 1366, and 'Unmannerly, uncivil, impolite; offensively or deliberately discourteous' particularly with regard to speech or actions, first recorded in 1386. The word derives from the Latin *rudis*: unwrought, unformed, inexperienced.

8 In the chant 'the referee's a Scouser/Geordie/Cockney', the identity of the opposing team determines the putative identity of the referee. The use of local and regional identity falls under the form of the 'blason populaire', a term coined by Auguste Canel in 1859 in his observations on customs in which people from Normandy lauded themselves and their own area while deriding others (see Gaidoz and Sébillot 1884). Contemporary football examples include 'we hate the Cockneys/Geordies/

Scousers', 'we all hate Mancs and Mancs and Mancs', 'Southerners, Southerners, Southerners'.

9   As with sexist chanting, homophobic abuse tends to be opportunistic and occasional rather than ritualized and part of the received repertoire; this is why it sounds more vicious and crude. It is often a response to tabloid news stories.

10 Raymond Williams describes structures of feeling as 'meanings and values as they are actively lived and felt' which have variable relations with formalized or systematic beliefs or codes; they are forms of practical consciousness which he refers to, significantly in this context, in terms of 'characteristic elements of impulse, restraint, and tone'. He cites the history of a language as the material location of changes in structures of feeling (Williams 1977: 132).

11 In fact this sense is misplaced since racist chanting does take place at England games, as for example in a game against Turkey in 2004. Though the chanting is now directed towards opposition players rather than black players in an England shirt, the national side is still a focus for racists.

References

Bourdieu, P. (1992) *Language and Symbolic Power*, Cambridge: Polity.

Gaidoz, H. and Sébillot, P. (1884) *Blason populaire de la France*, Paris: Cerf.

Harrison, T. (1989) *V.*, 2nd edn, Newcastle upon Tyne: Bloodaxe Books.

Masterman, C. F. G. (1902) *From the Abyss: Of Its Inhabitants: By One of Them*, London: Johnson.

Welsh, I. (1993) *Trainspotting*, London: Secker and Warburg.

Williams, R. (1977) *Marxism and Literature*, Oxford: Oxford University Press.

Chapter 9

Redefining rudeness

From polite social intercourse to 'good communication'

Deborah Cameron

Some years ago, when home-grown daytime TV talk shows on the model of *Oprah* were still relatively new in Britain, there was a minor scandal when the researchers on one show were accused of booking actors to impersonate 'ordinary people'. Their defence was intriguing: they claimed that there were simply not enough British people able to 'talk the talk-show talk'. Britons had not been socialized to 'let it all hang out', parading their problems publicly and showing uncontrolled emotion. Rather their ideas about appropriate behaviour centred on reticence, self-effacement, emotional continence and avoidance of offensive or embarrassing topics. As the supply of 'ordinary' exhibitionists ran out, the researchers had resorted to actors: people professionally trained to emote convincingly in front of an audience.

In the relatively short time that has elapsed since this incident, the problem appears to have resolved itself. Not only do British talk shows like *Trisha* continue to flourish (without, we must assume, relying on the services of actors), reality shows like *Big Brother* and *Wife Swap* have no trouble recruiting participants who have long since abandoned, if indeed they ever had any time for, the traditional British virtues of modesty and reserve. Rebecca Loos, a woman who came to public notice following an affair with the footballer David Beckham, extended her fifteen minutes of fame by masturbating a boar on a reality show called *The Farm*; *Big Brother* made a national celebrity of a contestant named Jade Goody, who personifies the stereotype of the ignorant and loud-mouthed 'chav' (a derogatory term applied to working-class British people, comparable to the American 'trailer trash'). Predictably, commentators have bemoaned the indecorousness of reality TV and its coarsening effect on British culture. But arguably TV is more a symptom than a cause, and it is certainly not where the rot, if it is one, started. I will return in due course to its other sources and manifestations, but first I must clarify my focus in this discussion, and place my argument in a broader historical context.

My focus in what follows will be specifically on the norms which are taken to govern verbal interaction, particularly though not exclusively in public (non-intimate and non-domestic) contexts. I will not be concerned with such non-linguistic manifestations of indecorousness as Rebecca Loos's TV pig-masturbating. Nor will I be concerned with the kind of linguistic indecorousness that is manifested in the use of rude or taboo words (a topic addressed in other chapters of this volume). I am interested, rather, in the rules of what the Victorians called 'social intercourse' – in what are considered to be an individual's rights and obligations when he or she interacts verbally with other individuals. My argument, in a nutshell, is that since the 1960s, and more precipitately since the beginning of the 1990s, there has been a sea-change in the way those rights and obligations are conceptualized. One result is that certain ways of interacting that were previously considered in British society to be socially inappropriate and 'rude' have come to be seen as unremarkable, or even preferable to more traditional ways of conducting a conversation.

Among the key actors promoting this shift are a new cadre of experts on 'good', 'effective' or 'skilled' communication. Notice I do not say these people are experts on 'politeness'. In the eighteenth, nineteenth and early twentieth centuries, the authorities to whom people turned for advice were concerned above all to define the rules of polite conversation; today, however, politeness is no longer considered the highest value to which a 'communicator' should aspire. That, indeed, is one of the most important elements in the 'sea-change' I have just alluded to. But it does not follow that today's experts are recommending 'rude' behaviour, even though that is how at least some of their recommendations are often perceived. In the technical sense in which linguists use the term 'politeness', the new orthodoxy of 'good communication' champions a certain kind of polite behaviour. But this is a different kind of politeness from the one that traditionally prevailed in Britain. To make the point clearer, we must delve a little deeper into the way linguistic politeness has been theorized.

The sociolinguistics of politeness (and rudeness)

In the most influential theory of politeness elaborated by sociolinguists and other social scientists (the classic reference for linguists is Penelope Brown and Stephen Levinson's 1987 monograph *Politeness*), 'being polite' is defined as a special way of treating people which displays the speaker's concern for their 'face' (the term is taken from the work of the sociologist Erving Goffman, and means much what it does in the expressions 'to lose face' and 'to save face'). In Brown and Levinson's model there are two kinds of face: 'positive face' (the desire of every person to be liked or approved of by others) and 'negative face' (the desire of every person to be free from unwanted impositions). Many or most of the acts we perform in everyday conversation are potentially threatening to one or both of these faces, either our own or our interlocutor's or both. Consequently, politeness phenomena are ubiquitous in our talk.

For instance, if I invite you to go out for a drink – not, you might think, a particularly delicate social negotiation – I am potentially threatening both your face and my own. Asking you to do something, in this case accompany me to the pub, is an imposition on you, which threatens your negative face. It also puts you in a position where if you do not want to come you will have to threaten my positive face, my need to be liked and approved of, by saying, in effect, 'I do not want the same thing you want'. How I handle this will depend on a number of factors. The key ones I have to consider are enumerated by Brown and Levinson as: the degree of imposition involved, the degree of intimacy or social distance between the parties, and whether there is a difference of rank or power. Inviting someone to the pub is low on imposition by contrast with, say, asking to borrow money from them, but it is more face-threatening if the person I am inviting is a stranger, or my boss, than if s/he is a close friend or a colleague of equal status. In any case, I will design my invitation in accordance with my perception of the threat. To a close friend I might say, 'Wanna go down the pub?', displaying no particular concern for face. To a stranger, however, I might use negative politeness, saying something like, 'You're probably too busy, but I was thinking that if you had time we could go for a quick drink'. This formulation (a) displays my understanding that I am imposing; (b) minimizes the imposition (e.g. by specifying a 'quick' drink); and (c) offers the recipient a graceful get-out – one that is not too threatening to my positive face, namely the idea of being 'too busy' – if s/he wants to say no. It also (d) displays a general intention to be polite by being couched very indirectly (conditional grammar, past tenses like 'I was thinking'). Although it contains no prototypical politeness formulas – 'please', 'thank you', 'sorry' and the like – this invitation is packed with linguistic markers of politeness.

Brown and Levinson argue (though the point has been disputed) that politeness operates on the same basic principles in every culture: what varies considerably across cultures, however, is the way people conventionally weight the variables of imposition, distance and power, and how they balance the claims of positive and negative face. In some cultures, for instance, any imposition on a person of higher rank calls for a degree of self-abasement that English speakers would regard as intolerably demeaning. In others, there is no need even to thank a friend who presents a gift to you, since such gift-giving is taken for granted rather than regarded as a special gesture. Many instances of cross-cultural misunderstanding and embarrassment result from ignorance or imperfect knowledge of these kinds of differences.

Traditional British politeness has been characterized in the terms of Brown and Levinson's model as essentially negative: based on avoidance of imposition, and weighted towards social distance. The quintessential British politeness formula might be 'excuse me', whose use among Britons displays sensitivity to even the smallest impositions – merely addressing someone or coming close to them may be seen to call for its utterance. Among older Britons it is not uncommon for people who have known one another for many years to go on using respect titles ('Mrs So-and-So') rather than first names, a practice which equates respect, even for one's equals, with keeping a certain distance. This contrasts with the politeness of mainstream US society, which is often said to be more positive, emphasizing closeness to others and friendly concern for their well-being. The quintessential American politeness formula, then, might be something like 'you're welcome', or 'you have a good day, now', both 'I-want-what-you-want' expressions which metaphorically stroke the other's positive face.

What are the implications of all this for our understanding of rudeness? Clearly, rudeness in interaction is not simply the absence of linguistic markers of politeness – it is not necessarily the case that non-polite formulations (like 'Wanna go down the pub?') are either intended or interpreted as rude. But context is important here. Rudeness can be inferred from the absence of politeness where such politeness would conventionally be expected (e.g. not uttering some expression of regret when you accidentally step on somebody's foot); it can also be inferred, however 'inaccurately' or 'unfairly', from the *presence* of a kind of politeness that is 'wrong' for the cultural context. For instance, in a culture which emphasizes protecting negative face by maintaining social distance, expressions of positive politeness like 'you have a good day, now' may be apprehended – even by speakers who know it is intended to be polite – as rude: intrusive, over-familiar, the verbal equivalent of standing too close. One culture's politeness may be another's rudeness.

'Culture' here, incidentally, does not always equate to 'nation': there may also be class, ethnic and gender differences in what is taken to be polite or rude. In the British case it is an interesting question how far recent developments reflect the influence of 'foreign' cultures – especially that of the USA – and how far they reflect shifts in the traditional relations between women and men, or between the working and the middle class. Before we consider that question, though, we must turn our attention to what these recent developments are, and how they have manifested themselves in Britain.

Changing norms: the evidence of advice literature

At the beginning of this chapter, discussing daytime talk shows and reality TV, I contrasted two sets of norms for social interaction: one I glossed as 'traditionally British' and another which I suggested was, in traditional terms, 'un-British', though increasingly it competes with the more traditional norm. Opposite I summarize the contrasts in Table 9.1.

The injunctions in the left-hand column are a distillation of the kind of advice that was standardly given by writers on etiquette and polite conversation from Victorian times to the late twentieth century – what might be called the 'social intercourse' tradition, in which talk was seen as like oil on a machine, lubricating social encounters and making them run smoothly. 'Politeness' in this tradition has two main elements. One is social decorum. There are conventional ways of speaking for any social occasion or setting, and it is incumbent upon participants to know and observe the relevant rules (a lot of advice literature during the period I am discussing was written to instruct the socially mobile or aspirant in the etiquette of situations that were not part of their

Table 9.1 Changing norms for social interaction

Traditional norm	Competing norm
Be reticent: don't monopolize talk or talk too much	Be articulate: self-expression is preferable to silence
Be self-effacing: don't talk about yourself, and especially don't boast	Be assertive: if you do not say who you are and show you value yourself, you can't expect others to recognize and respect you either
Be emotionally 'continent': keep your private feelings private, and if you must display them, do it without ostentation	Be emotionally 'literate': share your feelings with others, and be willing to listen without judging when they do the same
Be decorous: avoid topics or verbal acts that may shock, embarrass or offend	Be direct: 'difficult' topics need to be dealt with, not skirted round

formative social experience). The other element is the obligation to put others at their ease, taking account not only of the social situation but of individual interests and sensitivities. Etiquette writers recurrently stress that true politeness is not just a matter of outward social decorum, but must include this element of quasi-moral responsibility for the comfort of others.

The four injunctions I have listed are all points which recur when these writers explain how conversationalists can avoid breaching decorum and causing discomfort to their companions. It is evident that in substance these prescriptions and proscriptions support the contention that politeness, in British society (or 'Society'), traditionally emphasized avoidance and social distance. The ways of speaking to others which are censured here – talking too much, boasting about oneself, displaying strong emotions, and raising issues likely to elicit negative responses from others – transgress either the norm of not imposing (e.g. it is an imposition to make people listen to you for too long) or the norm of keeping your distance (e.g. by revealing your deepest emotions), or both. The implied ideal (though of course I am not claiming all or most British people actually instantiated it in their behaviour) resembles the familiar stereotype of the British as outwardly reserved, self-deprecating and undemonstrative, but kind and considerate underneath. This is essentially an upper- or middle-class stereotype, prototypically a male one (think of old war films and *Brief Encounter*) and until recently it was largely a positive one. The right-hand column of my table, however, shows the extent to which its positive connotations have been superseded by less positive ones.

I imagine that the ideal conversationalist – or as s/he is more usually labelled nowadays, 'communicator' – conjured up in the right-hand column will be thoroughly familiar to twenty-first-century readers, since the kind of advice literature in which this ideal is elaborated, variously labelled 'self-help', 'psychology', 'personal growth' or 'mind, body and spirit', now dominates the mass market. The 'social intercourse' tradition, whose leading exponents were qualified for the job largely by social experience, good taste and common sense, has been progressively displaced by this 'therapeutic' tradition, in which the experts are therapists and psychologists. They know more of the consulting room (and in some cases, the marital bedroom) than they do of the drawing room; and they do not see talk as oil for the wheels of social interaction, but rather as the *glue* we use for two interrelated purposes: sticking together coherent selves, and bonding with significant others.[1] From their point of view, the traditional British virtues of reticence, self-effacement, emotional continence and avoidance of conflict are not positive but on the contrary, unhealthy and dysfunctional. They say that these tendencies must be unlearned and replaced with others: articulacy, self-assertiveness, 'emotional literacy' (the ability to recognize and verbalize ('share') one's feelings) and a willingness to confront difficult issues or personal problems directly, undeterred by embarrassment or fear of offending others. The experts know very well that the kind of verbal behaviour they recommend was traditionally considered 'rude', and one recurring theme in their rhetoric is that we must stop seeing good manners as more important than good mental health. If that means abandoning the old norms of polite avoidance and distance, so be it.

The British talk show researchers, whose problems I began this chapter with, specifically mentioned as one reason for their difficulty in finding suitable 'ordinary people' to appear as guests the fact that few British people have ever been in therapy. The implication was that Americans knew how to 'talk the talk' because far more of them had direct experience of therapeutic practice. Actually, it might be more significant that Americans have had many more years of exposure to talk shows which, in their earlier and more staid (pre-*Jerry Springer*) incarnations, were both reflections of and advertisements for the therapeutic view of life and talk (Carbaugh 1988). But in any case, Frank Furedi (2004) has recently argued that the stereotype of Britain as particularly resistant to what he dubs 'therapy culture' is outdated: the values and practices associated with that culture have made significant inroads in Britain since the 1980s.

Though I agree with Furedi that this has happened, I do not think it has happened only or mainly because more British people are actually seeking therapy. The mass media are one influence, and education another (e.g. some British schools are now explicitly teaching 'emotional literacy' or 'emotional intelligence' (Goleman 1995)). But in my own view, the sphere where therapeutic notions of 'good communication' have achieved the most significant penetration is business and commerce. This is where the largest numbers of people have encountered what Furedi calls 'the therapeutic system of meaning', and where they have been impelled to engage with it most actively. Both as workers and as consumers (two roles which between them occupy large parts of most people's time and energy), millions of Britons are now required to treat ways of talking that they would once have seen as intrusive and 'rude' as normal and desirable. And at work, as opposed to in front of the TV, people are not just passive listeners. In many cases, it is a requirement of their jobs that they become fluent in certain kinds of therapy-speak themselves.

The corporate connection

In his 2002 BBC documentary series *The Century of the Self*, Adam Curtis drew attention to the strange alliance that arose between therapy and commerce in the late 1960s and 1970s. This was the time of the 'human potential' or 'personal growth' movement, beginning in the USA but soon spreading to other places, when all kinds of people with no clinical diagnosis sought self-improvement or enlightenment in various therapeutic practices. These being 'talking cures', they were conducted according to specific interactional conventions, some of which I have already mentioned (e.g. speak rather than be silent, share your feelings, listen without judging). In the context of something like group therapy it is entirely logical both to make rules for talking and to suggest that these particular rules are better suited to the purpose than other rules would be. But as the linguist Norman Fairclough (1992) argues, therapeutic rules for talking soon began to be treated as a 'discourse technology', a kind of tool-kit that could be applied in almost any context, even though in non-therapeutic contexts there was no compelling reason to follow these particular rules.

The diffusion of therapeutic rules for talking into non-therapeutic contexts began, as Curtis notes, when the originally counter-cultural practice of therapeutic self-improvement was seized on by its supposed enemy, corporate capitalism. Capitalists had perceived two things. First, they saw that the self-knowledge and self-expression advocated by the human potential movement could be harnessed for the purpose of stimulating consumption. Now that industry had got beyond the stage of 'any color you want so long as it's black', choosing and buying things could be portrayed as a way of expressing your individuality. Second, capitalists reasoned that if therapeutic techniques could make people happier in their personal lives, they might also be able to make happier and thus more productive workers. Large organizations like McDonald's took to training their managers in transactional analysis (the 'I'm OK, you're OK' technique developed by Eric Berne (1966)). Later on, companies would offer workers, as well as managers, 'communication training' based on therapeutic principles to help them in their dealings with one another and with customers. Today, this kind of communication training continues to be provided under new headings like 'teamwork' and 'customer care'. Few people in economically advanced societies, whether they work in the public or private sector, in services or in manufacturing, as managers or rank-and-file employees, have not by now had some kind of encounter with its principles. When capitalism went truly global following financial deregulation, and as first world economies became more and more dominated by service provision, the business version of therapy-speak became an international lingua franca.

It is difficult now to recall how alien this language sounded when it first became widespread in Britain. As late as 1998, when I was researching new workplace linguistic practices for a book (Cameron 2000), I discovered businesses which had had to abandon or modify the language of customer care because their customers regarded it as ludicrous or, indeed, rude. For instance, a supermarket in the Scottish town of Coatbridge decided to station a 'greeter' at the entrance to hand customers a basket and say 'Enjoy your shopping experience'. Customers responded with offended silence or derisive laughter; staff took to hiding in the toilets until they could be sure the greeter's job had been allocated to someone else. The initiative was quietly dropped. I also met a Scottish waitress who had resigned from her job at a hotel rather than follow a new management instruction to say 'Have a nice day' to guests. 'I found it demeaning to me as a Scot', she explained.

Another innovation many Britons on both sides of the counter disliked was the practice of using a customer's name at the checkout or in the bank, on the principle that customers will like you, and be loyal to your company, if it appears that you know them and take a personal interest in them. In practice, some people felt that the public announcement of their name was an intrusion on their privacy; others were irritated by the over-familiarity of servers who seemed to be claiming a personal relationship with them. In my research I found that many service workers shared the customers' perception of new practices as intrusive and/or disrespectful – in short, rude.

Today we have become more inured to these markers of what Norman Fairclough (1992) calls 'synthetic personalization' (i.e. performing impersonal and possibly scripted transactions in language designed to convey that one is treating the other as a unique and valuable individual). Several times in any given week, a complete stranger phoning me from a call centre in the hope of selling me something hails me by name and then asks me how I am, leaving a scripted pause for my reply; though I know, and s/he knows I know, that s/he could not give the proverbial damn. This kind of service-talk is no longer something the British remark on with outraged astonishment, as they often did when it was new; yet I suspect it still grates on many British ears. We do not care for false friendliness, and we still find some synthetic personalization techniques rude – intrusive, pushy, over-familiar. Also, we resent them for putting us in a position where we too will have to be rude. (Though I have sometimes wondered how many sales are made in Britain to people whose notions of decorum mean that they just cannot bring themselves to end phone calls unilaterally.)

Divided by a common language?

A recurring theme in this discussion has been cultural and linguistic differences between Britain and the USA, with the implication that what has been happening over the past two decades is a displacement of traditional British politeness norms by essentially American ones: these strike more conservative Britons as 'rude' because they are based on a 'foreign' notion of politeness, which stresses intimacy and concern for others rather than non-imposition and keeping a respectful distance. That would not be an entirely inaccurate account, but it is something of an over-simplification. The real source of new norms for communication is not the USA as a whole culture, but the institutions of therapy and certain forms of consumer capitalism. It is true that both are most entrenched in the USA, and are therefore easily seen as emanating from it (particularly in Britain where the shared language encourages organizations to import US products – from TV shows to workplace training materials – rather than producing British ones from scratch). But arguably the diffusion of new norms is less a consequence of American cultural influence *per se* than a consequence of the spread of the same social conditions which have enabled certain practices to flourish in the USA. If, for instance, British people have become less contemptuous than we used to be of therapy and the ways of talking it prescribes, it is less because of either desire or coercion to be 'like Americans' than because the need for therapy that has been answered there for decades is now also felt by many people here.

The historian Theodore Zeldin, discussing the 'social intercourse' tradition of writing about conversation, notes that Victorian writers considering what constituted 'good' talk accorded great importance to what I have called 'decorum', but were oddly unconcerned with 'the idea of personal contact, of the intimate meeting of minds and sympathies' (Zeldin 1998: 94). If this strikes contemporary readers as a curious lacuna, we might try to explain it in terms of the changing needs to which I have just referred. If facilitating 'the intimate meeting of minds' is now seen as the most important function of talk, whereas the Victorians treated it as peripheral or irrelevant, social theorists like Zygmunt Bauman (2000) and Anthony Giddens (1991) would argue that the shift is a logical response to the social transformations of the past few decades.

In Victorian times, most people's social ties were strong: few Britons moved more than a few miles from their birthplace during their lifetime, many households were large, jobs and marriages were for life (albeit many lives ended prematurely). Identity and intimacy were thus assured, for most people, by their embeddedness in stable social networks. Today, however, people are more mobile geographically and occupationally, households and families are smaller, and many relationships, including the most intimate ones, are conceived from the start as 'provisional' rather than permanent – when they cease to be satisfying, the parties will move on, unconstrained by the familial, economic and religious obligations of the past. Identity and intimacy, then, are no longer ready-made products of most people's life-circumstances; rather they become 'projects', things the individual must fashion and refashion over time. Talk is one of the most important tools we have to do this with, and the kinds of talk celebrated in therapy culture – the mutual emotional self-disclosure known as 'sharing', for example – are particularly important. In a world of strangers, 'sharing' is a condition for intimacy; in the view of Giddens, who regards therapy as a late modern 'technology of the self' rather than, say, a substitute for religion, verbalizing personal experience to either a therapist or a significant other serves the purpose of helping individuals who lead fragmented and discontinuous lives to sustain a coherent sense of identity.

I am suggesting, then, that what is driving the shift towards a 'therapeutic' view of 'good communication' is not the influence of American-style talk shows (our interest in them is symptomatic of deeper changes), or straight-forwardly of America itself, but the weakening of traditional social ties which began between the two world wars – not long after the Victorians – and has only really become general in Britain during the last 30 years. Other character-istics of and changes in British society may also be relevant. For instance, some commentators would argue that traditional accounts of British politeness behaviour have only ever in reality described the norms of the middle and upper classes: working-class British politeness is solidary rather than distance-based, and the norm of avoiding conflict or embarrassment is far weaker in working-class communities. While in my own view it is not possible to reduce class differences in Britain to such simple oppositions, it is undoubtedly true that differences exist; and one effect of the post-war breakdown in the old 'culture of deference' might be to make British society less inhospitable to certain norms of behaviour simply because they transgress middle-class standards – are 'rude' in the sense of 'uncultivated'. (Though the characterization of reality TV participants as 'chavs' suggests that snobbery is still one influence on British perceptions of rudeness.)

Another argument that has sometimes been made is that the triumph of a 'caring and sharing' interactional ethos reflects the growing feminization of British society. Certainly, new-style experts on communication tend to extol the virtues of women, while reserving their sternest warnings for stiff-upper-lipped British men. But as I have argued in more detail elsewhere (Cameron 2000, 2003), we should not be misled by the (coincidental) fact that therapeutic norms for interaction somewhat resemble the popular 'Mars and Venus' stereotype of the way women interact. It is not their 'femininity' but their utility in the conditions of late modernity (and especially for the purposes of late modern capitalism) which has caused these norms to be disseminated with such missionary zeal. Interestingly, too, their most skilful and successful British exponent is a man: his name is Tony Blair, and in the conclusion to this chapter I will consider the way he exploited new communicative norms at a key moment in recent British history.

Rudeness redefined: decorum and the death of Diana

All discussions of the demise of the British stiff upper lip must turn sooner or later to the unprecedented outbreak of nationwide public grief that occurred following the death of Princess Diana in a car accident in 1997. This is always cited as the moment when the British finally proved they had lost their traditional emotional inhibitions; it is less often mentioned in connection with the turn to rude or indecorous behaviour which is said to be coarsening our civic culture. Yet at the time, one significant public preoccupation involved a gladiatorial contest between 'old' and 'new' definitions of what is 'rude' in public utterance. This contest pitted the prime minister Tony Blair against the monarch, Queen Elizabeth II, both of whom made speeches to the nation.

Blair's speech, delivered apparently impromptu to TV cameras (though it later became clear he and Alastair Campbell had worked hard on it) was halting, full of long pauses, false starts and unstructured sentences that trailed off into incoherence; his delivery was emotional to the point of tearfulness. Though Blair did manage to get in some memorable sound-bites, the best-remembered being the assertion 'She was the People's Princess', essentially he gave the impression of a speaker rendered virtually inarticulate by the depth of his shock and grief. The Queen, on the other hand, delivered a clearly prepared and well-crafted speech in the manner of the traditional public eulogy. Though the matter included reference to shock and grief, the manner was more restrained: she spoke formally, articulating her periods with little visible or audible emotion, and certainly did not struggle to hold back tears.

The Queen observed the 'decorum' recommended by Victorian authorities: she responded to the occasion in the way traditionally considered fitting for that occasion. Tony Blair's response owed very little to that notion of decorous public utterance. An earlier generation might well have considered his inarticulacy, apparent lack of preparation and failure to control his emotions 'rude' – disrespectful to the audience, who were surely entitled on such a solemn occasion to expect something with more formality and substance, and also disrespectful to the memory of the Princess. Yet in 1997 it was the Queen rather than Blair who was judged by the British public to have disrespected Diana and the nation. Her emotional restraint was construed as a callous lack of real feeling; her formality and articulacy were contrasted unfavourably with Blair's inability to string a sentence together, which supposedly proved that his feelings were real and deep. From Blair the British felt they got what Theodore Zeldin glosses as 'the intimate meeting of minds and sympathies'; from the Queen they got only the proprieties, which many of them suspected were not a true reflection of her feelings.

In the age that emphasized decorum (the age to which the Queen in fact belongs), that suspicion would have been less damaging. The overriding duty of a 'decorous' speaker was to express the sentiments conventional to the occasion. In the event those sentiments did not correspond to the speaker's true feelings, it was better to be insincere than indecorous. But as Martin Montgomery (1999) points out in his analysis of the two speeches I have been discussing, today's audiences (and Tony Blair) belong to the television generation: they expect a more 'personal' mode of address, and are accustomed to scrutinizing speakers closely (since television can and does show them in close-up) with a view to assessing their emotional states. Modern audiences are also familiar with the 'therapeutic' injunction to 'share', which implies that insincerity – withholding or disguising what one 'really' thinks and feels – is a breach of the contract between speaker and hearer. Sincerity, not propriety or decorum, is the overriding duty of today's public figures, and the main criterion by which their public utterances are judged. Tony Blair instinctively understands that; the Queen has never learned it.

In the contrast between these two prominent Britons we see, once again, the difference between talk as oil, needed to lubricate the surfaces of social encounters, and talk as glue, needed to ensure 'the intimate meeting of minds and sympathies'. If talk is oil, some measure of insincerity is inevitable, and perhaps even indispensable; if it is glue, however, insincerity is destructive of the trust on which intimacy depends. Britain today seems to be a society in transition between these two understandings: the result is a shifting and variable notion of what is acceptable, desirable or 'rude' in spoken discourse.

Note

I owe the 'oil and glue' metaphor to the historian Michèle Cohen, whom I also thank for her many insights into the changing nature of conversation in the modern West.

References

Bauman, Z. (2000) *Liquid Modernity*, Cambridge: Polity.

Berne, E. (1966) *The Games People Play*, New York: Grove Press.

Brown, P. and Levinson, S. (1987) *Politeness: Some Universals in Language Use*, Cambridge: Cambridge University Press.

Cameron, D. (2000) *Good to Talk? Living and Working in a Communication Culture*, London: Sage.

——— (2003) 'Gender and Language Ideologies', in J. Holmes and M. Meyerhoff (eds) *The Handbook of Language and Gender*, Malden, MA: Blackwell.

——— (2006) 'Men are from Earth, Women are from Earth', in D. Cameron, *On Language and Sexual Politics*, London: Routledge.

Carbaugh, D. (1988) *Talking American: Cultural Discourse on Donahue*, Norwood, NJ: Ablex.

Curtis, A. (2002) *The Century of the Self*, London: BBC.

Fairclough, N. (1992) *Discourse and Social Change*, Cambridge: Polity.

Furedi, F. (2004) *Therapy Culture: Cultivating Vulnerability in an Uncertain Age*, London: Routledge.

Giddens, A. (1991) *Modernity and Self-Identity: Self and Society in the Late Modern Age*, Cambridge: Polity.

Goleman, D. (1995) *Emotional Intelligence*, New York: Bantam.

Montgomery, M. (1999) 'Speaking Sincerely: Public Reactions to the Death of Diana', *Language and Literature* 8: 5–33.

Zeldin, T. (1998) *Conversation: How Talk Can Change Your Life*, London: Harvill.

Index

Note: page numbers in *italics* denote illustrations

Abbott, T. 99
Abramovich, Roman 123
accents, regional 15, 56
acceptability: behaviour 120–1, 125n5;
    obscenity 96; *see also* value shifts
Adams, J. N. 51
Addison, Joseph 23
Adley, Robert 107
adultery 28–9
advertising: nudity 97; for package
    holidays 103; pornography 93, *94*, 95;
    Viz 90, 93, *94*, 95
Advertising Standards Authority 11
agitate 32
Alibhai-Brown, Yasmin 2
alvine 28
American Heritage Dictionary 9
American Tramp and Underworld Slang
    (Irwin) 41, 52
Anti-immigration Acts 103
anti-permissiveness 99
anti-racist strategies 124
Anti-Social Behaviour Orders 2
Antrim 58
anus 27, 92
Anzac 41, 42–3, 46, 49
archaism 28
Archer, Jeffrey 64
Armstrong, Nancy 3
Arne, Thomas Augustine 6
arse 8, 42–3
Atkinson, Ron 11
Aubrey, Anne 100
Auden, W. H. 73, 78
Australian English 35, 49; slang 36, 44,
    47; *see also* Partridge, Eric

Australian National Dictionary
    (Macquarie) 35–6

Bailey, Nathaniel 24, 27, 31
ballocks 50
Barnes, John 124
barrikin 47
basin 29–30
Bauman, Zygmunt 135
BBC3 9
Beano 82, 85
Beckham, David 123, 127–8
behaviour, acceptable 120–1, 125n5
Belfast 56; male bonding 59; street song
    61; vernacular language 56–7, 58; *see
    also* Ulster words
Bell, Steve 91
'Beluncle,' *New Statesman* 8–9
Bennett, J. A. 40
Berne, Eric 133
Big Brother 127
black football players 123–4
black women 103–4
Blackpool 76
Blaikie, Thomas 2
Blair, Tony 2, 17, 115, 136, 137–8
blason populaire 125–6n8
bloody 11, 43
*Bloomsbury Dictionary of Contemporary
    Slang* 36
bog 28
Bourdieu, Pierre 117–18, 125n1
Boyes, Karen 105
Bragg, Billy 100
breastfeeding in public 108
Brief Encounter 131

Brighton 74
Brighton Football Club 123
Britain, Romans in 6–7
Britannia: authority 5–6; freedom 5;
   Roman conquest 6–7; Rowlandson
   4–5; versions 1–2, 3, 7; see also 'Rude
   Britannia: A Nation Transformed'
British Broadcasting Corporation 11
British Empire 6
Britishness 2, 6
Broadcasting Standards Commission 10,
   11
Broadcasting Standards Council 116
Brookes, Richard 43
Brophy, John 41, 52
brothel 43
Brown, Penelope 13, 128, 129
Browning, Robert 31
Brownlow, Jim 82, 83, 84, 86
bugger 40, 52
Bull, John 3–4, 14
bum chain 92
bumf 44
Burchfield, R. W. 9, 25, 33, 40, 48, 53–4n4
Burns, Robert 42
Burton, Sir Richard 42
Bush, George W. 125n2
business world: communication 132–3,
   136; therapeutic tradition 133–4

call centres 134
Callaghan, James 99
Cameron, Deborah 16–17, 134
Campbell, Alastair 115, 137–8
Canadian military slang 47
Canel, Auguste 125–6n8
cant words 47–8
capitalism: consumer 135; late modern
   136
carnivalesque 93, 120
Carry On films 93, 101
Carter, Angela 53n1
Cassell's Dictionary of Slang 36
Cawdrey, Robert 24, 29, 32
celebrity 2
censorship 9–10, 15, 97
Cervantes, Miguel de: Don Quixote 77–8
Channel 4 116
Charles II 4
Chaucer, Geoffrey 79–80
chav 3, 127, 136
Chelsea football club 123

Cheney, Dick 125n2
childer 60
Chippindale, Peter 98
Christ 11
Churchill, Winston 106–7, 108–9, 110
civility in decline 2; see also politeness
class: deference 2; deviancy 12;
   eighteenth century 13–14; language
   12–13, 118–20; politeness 13, 14; see
   also middle class; working class
class war 116–17
A Classical Dictionary of the Vulgar
   Tongue (Grose) 24, 41–2
Cleethorpes 74
Coatbridge 134
cock 8, 31
Cockney rhyming slang 43, 47
Coleman, John 78
colloquialism 45–6
colonial language 44, 48–9
colonial racism 104
come 40
comedy, low 93
Comfort, Alex 74
commonness 3, 12, 78
communication 128, 132–3, 136
Concise Oxford Dictionary 91
condom 30, 32
coney 32
conformity in language 118–19
consumer capitalism 135
contagion of language 23
'The Contrast' (Rowlandson) 4–5
control: desire 3; female body 3;
   imperial 6
Cook, William 89
Cooke, Kaz: The Crocodile Club 35, 36,
   37, 53n1
Cool Britannia 115
copulation 28, 41
Cory, William 26
Cosmopolitan 101, 108
Crick, Bernard 73
crime, drink-related 2
Crime and Disorder Act (1998) 2
The Crocodile Club (Cooke) 35, 36, 37,
   53n1
Crowley, Tony 16
Cruickshank, George 79
Crumb, Robert 83
Cudlipp, Hugh 101
culture: European differences 102; as

polite learning 14; politeness 130;
   rudeness 2, 14–15
cunnilingus 36, 40
Cunningham, Valentine 15
cunt: Broadcasting Standards 11; *coney*
   32; in dictionaries 9, 30; *Lady*
   Chatterley's Lover 8, 52; Lawrence 8,
   38, 52; sexism 91
Curtis, Adam 133

Daily Express 2, 116
Daily Mail 2, 86
Daily Mirror 97; *see also* Mirror
Dali, Salvador 73, 77
damn 11
Dandy 85
daub 23
Davin, Dan 9, 40, 53–4n4
Davis, Norman 40
Day, Venetia 103
decency 90–1
decorum: Diana 136–8; Elizabeth II 17,
   137, 138; Johnson 23–4; Latin 27;
   social intercourse 130–1, 135
deference 2
deltiology 73, 80n1
Denison, C. 40–1
Desailly, Marcel 11
desire, regulation of 3
deviancy 12
devolution 6
dialect 8, 15; *see also* Wright, Joseph
Diana, Princess 17, 136–8
Dickens, Charles: Artful Dodger 45;
   comic writing 79; *David Copperfield*
   48; *Great Expectations* 47; *Household*
   Words 48–9; *The Pickwick Papers* 26;
   prostitutes 48
Dictionary of Australian Colloquialisms
   (Wilkes) 52–3
Dictionary of Forces' Slang (Granville,
   Roberts and Partridge) 47
Dictionary of RAF Slang (Joseph) 47
Dictionary of Slang and Unconventional
   English (Partridge) 44–5, 49, 53
Dictionary of the English Language
   (Johnson) 23–4
A Dictionary of the Underworld
   (Partridge) 47
digger 41
Diggerspeak 51–2
disremember 66

Dixon, James 32
Dobson, Eric 40
Dolan, Terry 58
Donald, Chris: adverts 90; Enterprise
   Allowance 82; *Loaded* interview 93; as
   outsider 84; parody 90; Profanisaurus
   92; punk influences 89; *Rude Kids* 83;
   starting *Viz* 82–3
Donald, Simon 82, 83, 84, 89, 92
doubles entendres 74, 78, 88
drunk, words for 63
dunny 53
Dury, Graham 83

Eastbourne 74
Ecclesiastes 78–9
education 125n4
Egerson, F. C. C. 44
Elizabeth II: decorum 17, 137, 138;
   Mirren as 99
Elliot, Michael 2
emotional literacy 132
Encarta World English Dictionary 27, 29
English Dialect Dictionary (Wright) 40,
   41
English language, US/British 134–6
etiquette 130–1
euphemism 28, 29, 30, 37
Evans, Gillian 12
excrement 28
Exeter Assizes 27
expostulate 32
eyewash 44

Fairclough, Norman 133, 134
The Fall 92
Fanshawe, Simon 2
Fardell, John 84
The Farm 127
Farmer, John 24, 30–1, 32, 42
fart 23–4
Fat Slags 3, 5, 91, 93
fatness 3
fellatio 40
female body 3
feminism 100
Fenton, James 58
FHM 93
filth 48
Financial Times 12
finger gesture 1
Florio, John 42

football 120, 123–4
football chants: changes 16; formulaic
    121; homophobia 123; identity 122;
    non-racist 123–4; parody 122;
    performativity 121–2; racism 120,
    126n11; violence 120; witticisms 122–3
football supporters: acceptable behaviour
    120–1; homophobia 126n9; Liverpool
    122, 125n3, 125n6; rudeness 121, 122;
    speech acts 120; *v.* 115–18
fottere 42
foutre 51
Fox, Sam 106
France 97, 103
Frear, Steven 17
French letter 40
frig 40
Fryer, Peter 25, 29
fuck: Broadcasting Standards
    Commission 11; dictionary entry 9,
    24, 40; etymology 42; *Lady
    Chatterley's Lover* 7–8, 52; Lawrence
    7–8, 38, 52; Murray 32; in newspapers
    10; Tynan 9–10, 82; *Viz* 90
fur pie 36
furbelow 49
furburger 35–6
fur-doughnut 36
Furedi, Frank 132
Furnivall, Frederick 25
furphies 44, 49, 50–1
Furphy, John 49
furry hoop 36

Garland, Nicholas 35
Gatrell, Vic 14
gay men 106; *see also* homophobia
gender 16
Ghandi, Indira 125n2
Giddens, Anthony 135, 136
Gillray, James 5
God 11
Goffman, Erving 128
Goody, Jade 127
Goram, Andy 122
Granville, Wilfred 47
Gray, Douglas 40
Green, Jonathon 36, 49–50
greeters 134
Griffith-Jones, Mervyn 8
Grose, Francis 24, 41–2, 47, 50
Grundy, Bill 82

Guardian 91
Guthrie, Sir Tyrone 60

Habermas, Jürgen 13
Hair 97
hair-pie 36
Hall, Lesley 26
Hall, Michael 53n1
Hansard 106
Harmony Week 103
Harrison, Tony 125n4; V. 115–18, 123
Haste, Cate 106
Hawkins, Desmond 73
Health and Efficiency 97
Heaney, Seamus: 'Broagh' 57, 59, 60
Heath, Ted 115
Hell's Angels 100
Henley, W. E. 24, 42
Herbert, A. P. 79
Hillsborough 120, 125n6
Hobbes, Thomas 25
homophobia 123, 126n9
Hopkins, G. M. 56–7, 66
Horizon 71, 73–4
Horrie, Chris 98
hot stuff 41
Housman, A. E. 73
Howarth, Gerald 116
hump 41
Humphries, Barry 35

identity 122; *see also* national identity
I'm a Celebrity Get Me Out of Here!
    10
immigration 103
imposition, social 128–9
Indecent Displays Bill 105
Indecent Displays (Control) Act 107
Independent 2
Independent Television Commission 11
indescribables 26
ineffables 26
Inman, Andy 89
innuendo 88
Institute of Communication Studies 10
insults 11
intimacy 129, 135, 138
Iraq war 90
Irwin, Godfrey 41

Jackie 86
jakes 44

Jenkins, Roy 99
jig-a-jig 41
Johnny Fartpants 84, *85*
Johnson, Samuel 23–4, 25, 33
Jones, Davey 85–6, 92
Joseph, Michael 47
Joyce, James: *Ulysses* 42, 51
Jura, Isle of 71, 73

Kick Racism Out Of Football campaign
    124
Kissinger, Henry 125n2
knocking shop 41

Lacan, Jacques 36–7, 48
ladette 3, 5
Lads' Mags 93–4
Lady Chatterley's Lover (Lawrence) 7–8,
    38, 42, 52, 82
Laird, Andrew 64–5
Lakoff, R. 13
Lamb, L. 96, 98, 100, 101, 104
language: class 12–13, 118–20;
    colonialism 44, 48–9; conformity
    118–19; contagion 23;
    legitimate/illegitimate 119–20; rude
    12–13, 115; social constraints 118,
    119–20; social power 118; strong 10;
    taboo 7–8; vernacular 56–7, 58;
    vulgarity 24; working class 118–19
Larkins, Philip 7–8
Latin language 27, 31
latrine 44
latrine rumour 41, 44, 50
latrine talk 53
Laugesen, Amanda 49
lavatories 29
lavatory humour 83
Lawrence, D. H. 8, 51; *Lady Chatterley's
    Lover* 7–8, 38, 42, 52, 82
Le Saux, Graeme 123
Leavis, F. R. 8
Leech, G. N. 13
lesbianism 29
Levinson, Stephen 13, 128, 129
Levy, Ariel 93
lexicography 9, 24
Lexicon totius Anglicitatus (Trench) 33
Lindstrom, Ulla 102
linguistic capital 118, 121
Literary Sessions (Eric Partridge Ltd) 43
Little Britain 3, 4

Liverpool football supporters 122, 125n3,
    125n6
Llewelyn-Bowen, Laurence and
    Jacqueline 2
Loaded 93
Locke, John 23, 24
loins 26–7
Loncraine, Rebecca 16
Longford Report 104–5
Loos, Rebecca 127–8
Lusardi, Linda 106
Lydon, John 10
Lyon, Alexander 105

Macafee, Caroline 58
McDonald's 133
McGill, Donald: background 74;
    examples 71–3; Orwell on 16, 73–4,
    76, 92; prosecuted 75–6; subversiveness
    80
McKenzie, Barry 35
MacKenzie, Kelvin 102, 106
Macquarie's *Australian National
    Dictionary* 35–6
MacSharry, Deirdre 96
Magwitch, Abel 47–8
Major, John 64–5, 115
male bonding 59
Manchester United 125n6
manners 2; *see also* politeness
Manning, Frederic 42–3
marginalized social groups 13, 40, 116–17
Masterman, C. E. G. 119
masturbate 33
Maxim 93
Mayhew, Sir Patrick 65
media 100, 116
Megarry, Robert 102
menstruation 27–8
Middle English plurals 60
middle-class 3, 14, 130; *see also* class
militarisms, slang 45–6
Mill, John Stuart 6
mill girls 63
Miller, Henry: *Tropic of Cancer* 76
Miller, Max 78
Mirren, Helen 99
Mirror 2, 98, 101
misogyny 96
Mitchell, Bruce 40
modesty 3
Montgomery, Martin 137–8

Moore, Bruce 36
morality 116
motherfucker 11
muff 36
Mugglestone, Lynda 15
Muldoon, Paul: 'Quoof' 57–8
Munro, Linda 105
Murdoch, Rupert 97, 98, 106
Murray, James 27, 30, 32

names: Magwitch 47–8; over-familiarity 134; social stereotyping 12
National Front 103
National Geographic 104
national identity 1–2, 3, 6, 7, 14
naturism 97
naughtiness 16
Nesbitt, Darren 100
Neville, Richard 53–4n4
A New English Dictionary on Historical Principles 25
New Statesman 8–9
New Zealand 40, 44, 52–3
News of the World 98
newsagents 71–3, 74
nigger 11, 91
Nixon, Richard 125n2
Noel-Tod, Jeremy 91
nudity: advertising 97; black women 103–4; European women 102; French women 102; male 101–2; public 97, 106–7; *see also Sun*

Obermeier, Uschi 98, 102
Obscene Publications Acts 7–8, 75, 106, 110
obscenity: acceptability 96; demeaning women and sex 106–7; dialect 8; Orwell 76; paternalism 8; subversive 79–80; *Viz* 90–1; vulgarity 79
O'Connell, Daniel 64
Ofcom (Office of Communications) 10
Oh! Calcutta! 97
Old English plurals 60
Old Norse words 64
Oprah 127
orgasm 28
O'Rourke, Mary 125n2
Orwell, George: 'The Art of Donald McGill 73–4, 92; 'Boys' Weeklies' 71–2; Ecclesiastes 78–9; 'Funny, But Not Vulgar' 79; 'Inside the Whale'

76–7; low comedy 93; McGill postcards 16, 73–4, 76, 92; Miller 78; *Nineteen Eighty-Four* 79; obscenity 76, 77; Powell 71; Sancho Panza 77–8; spoken/printed word 82
over-familiarity 130, 134
Oxford English Dictionary: Additions Series 16; *basin* 29–30; rude words 15; scientific language 28; *Supplement* 25–6, 33, 40; swear words 82; Trench 24–5
OZ magazine 9, 53–4n4

package holidays 103
Page Three girls, *Sun* 16; as figurehead 96; mummy-babies 105–7; origins of 98–9; pornography 104–5; publicity 97, 105–7; racism 103–4; Short 108–10; types of women 101–4; violence against women 100
Paine, Thomas 5
Paisley, Ian 64–5
Paki 11, 91
parody: football chants 122; *Viz* magazine 90
Partridge, Eric 15; American slang 41; Australian slang 35, 39–40; background 37–8; *Dictionary: latrine rumour* 50; *Dictionary of Forces' Slang* 47; *Dictionary of Slang and Unconventional English* 44–5, 49, 53; *A Dictionary of the Underworld* 47; *Literary Sessions* 43; New Zealand 40; scholarly back-stories 42–3; *Shakespeare's Bawdy* 51; *Slang To-Day and Yesterday* 44; soldier-speak 40–1; *Songs and Slang of the British Soldier* 51–2; *For These Few Minutes* 46–7; *Words, Words, Words!* 43–4; *Words at War* 47
Pascoe, David 16
paternalism 8
Paulin, Tom: *A New Look at the Language Question* 58; Ulster words 15, 58–67
Paxman, Jeremy 14
Penguin Books 7–8
Penguin English Dictionary 9
penis 31
Pepys, Samuel 4–5
performativity 121–2
permissive society 2, 8, 96, 98, 106

personal growth movement 133
personalization, synthetic 134
pferfies 41, 50
picture postcards 16, 71–3, 74; *see also*
    McGill, Donald
piece 41, 63, 67
pimp 43
piss 8, 23–4
pistol 51
Playboy 95, 100
poetry in vernacular 57, 117
Poitier, Sidney 103
polite society 13–17
politeness: absence of 130; class 13, 14;
    communication 128; culture 13–15,
    23–6, 130; Johnson 23–4; linguistic 30,
    32; national identity 14; prudish 12;
    sociolinguistics 128–30; traditional
    British 129–30
politicians 11, 107, 115, 138
Pollard, Vicky 3, *4*
pornography: Longford Report 104–5;
    picture postcards 73; soft 106; *Viz* 93,
    94, 95; *see also* Page Three girls, *Sun*
postcards: *see* picture postcards
Poubelle, Eugène 36–7
poubellication (Lacan) 36–7, 48
Poultner, Thomas, and Sons 30–1
Powell, Anthony 71, 73
Powell, Enoch 103
press, freedom of 96, 110
Private Eye 35, 89
privy 30
procurer 43
Profanisaurus 89, 90, 92
pronunciation, Elizabethan 56–7
Proops, Marje 98, 101
Prospect 2
prostitution 29, 33, 43, 48
prudery 25
public discourse 17, 115
pump ship 41
Punch 27, 89
punk 89

The Queen (Frear) 17, 99

Rabelais, François 44
Race Relation Acts 103, 124
racial abuse 11, 91
racial equality, *Sun* 103–4
racism: absence 123–4; colonial 104;

football chants 120, 126n11; Page
    Three girls 103–4
rape stories 100
Ratcliffe, S. 102
reality television shows 127, 136
refinement 3
religious terms of abuse 11
respect 129–30
respectability 3
restraint 92, 137
reticence 16, 23, 132
Reynolds, Albert 125n2
Rhan, Stephanie 98, 102, 103
rhyming slang 43, 47
Roberts, Frank 47
Rolling Stones 98, 101
Romans in Britain 6–7
roti 67
Rotten, Johnny 10
Rougiers, postcard sellers 73
Rowlandson, Thomas: 'The Contrast'
    4–5
Royal Military College Duntroon 36
Rubens, Peter Paul 91
rude 7, 125n7
'Rude Britannia: A Nation Transformed'
    1–2, 3, 6, 7
Rude Kid jokes 86–7
rude language: class 12–13; *OED* 15;
    public use 115
rudeness: absence of politeness 130;
    changing 10, 16–17, 124; culture 2,
    14–15; football supporters 121, 122;
    gender 16; national identity 1–2;
    picture postcards 16; politicians 107,
    115; sociolinguistics 128–30; *Viz* 16,
    89; working class 121
'Rule Britannia' (Thomson) 6
Russell, Ken 99

sanitation 29
satire 84
Scargill, Arthur 116
schoolboy humour 89
scientific language 27–8
Scottish workers 134
screw 41
scrotum 28
scrounge 41
scurvy 43
seaside towns 74–6
Sex Pistols 10, 82, 89

sexism 91, 123
sexuality 30–1, 33
shabby 25
shag 41
Shakespeare, William 44; *Cymbeline* 60;
  Hamlet 63; *Henry IV, Part 1* 63; *Henry
  IV, Part 2* 51; Partridge 51
sharing 135–6, 138
Shelden, Michael 76
Shifrin, Sue 100
shit 8, 50
shit, talking 50
shite 50
Short, Clare 105, 106–7; *Sun* 108–10
Shorter Oxford English Dictionary 9
silenced people 116–18, 119–20
sincerity 138
Sisam, Kenneth 40
slang 35–6; Australian 39–40, 44;
  Canadian 47; military 45–6, 47; New
  Zealand 44; *see also* Partridge, Eric
Slang and its Analogues (Farmer and
  Henley) 24, 30
slang dictionaries 9, 15, 36, 37
slut 11
Smith, Mark E. 92
Smith, Minerva 103
snobbery 136
social constraints 118, 119–20
social distance 129–30
social intercourse: British/un-British
  130–2; decorum 130–1, 135; Victorian
  128
social status 3; *see also* class
social stereotyping 12
sociolinguistics 128–30
soldier-speak 40–1
Sowery Bridge 104
Spanish football 124
step on a duck 92
Stewart, Frances, Duchess of Richmond 4
Straw, Jack 2
street song 61
Stuff 93
subversiveness 79–80
Suckling, Sir John 23
Sun: adverts for package holidays 103;
  circulation wars 98; female readership
  101; Irish editions 98; Longford Report
  104–5; moral uncertainty 99; offence
  104; publicity 97, 104, 105–7; racial
  equality 103–4; Short 108–10;

Thatcherism 106; violence against
  women 100; women's pages 101; *see
  also* Page Three girls
Sunday Times Magazine 97
swear words: OED 82; Ofcom 10; public
  82; sexual 90; *Viz* 86
Sweary Mary 87
Swift, Jonathan 23; *Gulliver's Travels*
  79–80
syphilis 43

Table Alphabeticall (Cawdrey) 24, 29, 32
taboo: bodily functions 12; changing 11,
  92, 96–7; euphemism 29; lexicography
  9, 24; literature 7–8; naughtiness 16
tail 41
Tait, Theo 16
talk show, television 127, 132
tart 11
Taylor, D. J. 74
Taylor, Teddy 116
tegument 28
Telegraph 1
Tennenhouse, Leonard 3
Tennyson, Alfred 59
Thackeray, W. M. 79
Thames Today 82
Thatcher, Margaret 105, 107
Thatcherism 106, 115–16, 117
Theatre Act (1968) 97
therapeutic tradition 132, 133–4, 135, 136
therapy-speak 132–3
Thomson, James 6
Thorne, Tony 36
Thorp, Simon 83, 88
Times 97
Times Literary Supplement 25, 52
toilet 29
topless sunbathing 97, 102
Trench, Richard Chenevix 24–5, 27, 32–3
tribade 29, 33
Trisha 127
trousers 26
Truss, Lynne 2–3
twat 31
Tynan, Kenneth 9–10, 82

Ulster words 15, 56–7, 58–67
United States of America 36, 41
Universal Etymological Dictionary
  (Bailey) 24, 31
unmentionables 26

urinate, words for 41, 64
Urquhart, Sir Thomas 44

vagina 36
value shifts 3, 96–7, 99; *see also* Victorian values
vernacular: Belfast 56–7, 58; in poetry 57, 117
Vickers, Sally 108
Victorian values 25–6, 32–3, 105
violation 29
violence against women 100
Viz 82; advertising pornography 93, *94, 95*; characters 3, 5, 82, *83–5, 87, 88*; obscenity 90–1; parody 86, 90; rudeness 16, 89; swearing 86
vulgarity 2, 24, 76, 79, 89
vulva 28

Watch Committees 74–6
water-closet 30
Watford, Alex 97
Watts, Richard J. 13, 14
Waugh, Auberon 89
Webster's Third New International Dictionary 9
Weekley, Ernest 38, 41

Weeks, J. 33
Welsh, Irvine 125n4; *Trainspotting* 118–19
Weymouth 74
Whitehouse, Mary 106
whore 91
Wife Swap 127
Wilkes, G. A.: *Dictionary of Australian Colloquialisms* 52–3
Williams, Bernard 6
Williams, Raymond 11, 54n4, 126n10
Williamson, Fred 103
Wilson, Harold 115
Windsor, Barbara 101
Wodehouse, P. G. 79
working class: education 125n4; language 118–20; Lawrence 9; rudeness 121; Thatcherism 116; *see also* class
Wright, Joseph: *English Dialect Dictionary* 40, 41

Yalom, Marilyn 97, 108
'You'll Never Walk Alone' 122

Zeldin, Theodore 135, 137